Puppies from Heaven

Susan Luginbuhl

Llumina Press

Some names in the book have been changed to protect privacy

ISBN: 978-1-59526-817-4

Printed in the United States of America by Llumina Press

Library of Congress Control Number: 2007903444

Dedicated to My Mother
Whose Support and Encouragement
Made This Book a Reality

Chapter 1

The shrill ringing of the telephone shattered the early morning quiet. I grabbed the receiver, hoping someone was calling about a dog.

"Are you the people that raise dogs, umm, I mean Labs?" a trembling voice asked.

"Why yes, that's us," I volunteered cheerfully. "I have some pups available too."

"Oh!" the voice gasped, "I just have to have a dog right now!" I could hear the woman's thin voice start to break. "We had a Lab, and she was only six months old and she died yesterday while she was being spayed," the woman explained, her voice choking as she began to cry, deep, heart-wrenching sobs sounding in my ear.

"Tell me about it," I urged as gently as I could.

"Oh, she was the best dog in the world. We loved her so much."

The tears began again, and I waited quietly. "My husband and I don't have any children, and this dog, Lacy her name is, I mean was, she was our whole life. We taught her so many things. We never ever imagined there was even a chance she could die during the surgery or we would have never had it done, you know." She stopped for a moment and I could hear her blowing her nose. "We took her to the vet's in the morning. He called at noon and said...and said that she was dead. Said it happens every once in a while—a reaction to the anesthesia or something. Oh, I just feel so awful!" she ended, and the sobs began again in earnest.

"Why that's terrible," I murmured, frowning as I imagined how I would feel if one of my own beloved dogs had died during a common, almost routine, surgery.

"Do you have any black girls?" she managed to ask. "Lacy, she was all black, and well, I'd like to get one just like her if I could, you know."

"I understand completely," I said nodding my head. "You aren't going to believe this, but I do have one black female left." I smiled as I glanced down at the small silky pup curled up by my feet on the kitchen floor. "She's a cutie, and we have her parents here so you can..."

"Oh, you do?" she broke in hurriedly. "Can I come over right now? I mean as soon as I stop crying, that is. I've been crying all night and I can hardly see straight." Her words tumbled out jerkily. "I saw your ad in the paper this morning, and I had cried so much, and my eyes were so bleary that I wondered if I had even dialed the right number. Oh, I'm so glad I called you!" She paused to blow her nose again.

"Well," I hesitated, "I should tell you how much my pups are. The price is..."

"Oh, I don't care about the price," she cut in disdainfully. "I *need* a dog," she whispered softly. "And I don't care what it costs. I just have to have one."

So starts another day in the life of a dog breeder, I mused as I hung up the phone. It had been many years since we purchased our first shiny black Labrador Retriever. We named her Licorice after our four sons' favorite candy. I convinced Rick, my skeptical, but wonderfully tolerant husband, that we should breed Licorice and have just one litter of pups so our boys could see puppies being born. After all, it was educational, wasn't it? Now here we were, years later, still raising puppies.

After that first lively litter of ten puppies had been born in the coat closet off the dining room, I found that I had fallen in love with the whole process. It seemed to bring out my possessive maternal instincts. They were not only Licorice's pups, but mine too. While she panted in hard, intense labor, I hunkered down right beside her, breathing pretty hard myself.

I cried when I sold the first pup. It almost seemed as though I was selling one of my own children. I inadvertently made the wonderful family who was buying that first pup feel so guilty that after picking it out, they promptly handed it back to me and said, "You better carry it up to the house; we can see this is awfully hard on you." Then they proceeded to ask me, after they had bought and paid for the pup, if they could go now. They wanted to make sure I would be all right. Bless their hearts!

We ended up keeping a lively yellow girl named Trixie from that first litter, and additional pups from subsequent litters. Many a mealtime was and is spent with Rick and me discussing who's in heat at the moment, who's not keeping their pen clean at night, how many pups our next mom might have, which expectant mom is bagging up, and so on. It never occurred to me to wonder how our boys felt about the unusual table conversation. Needless to say, they have had a varied, and for the most part, interesting, canine education through the years, whether they realized it or not at the time.

Today we have ten adult Labs that make their home with us, and numerous puppies that come and go. While it remains for the most part "my business," my husband does hold the unglamorous, but very important, title of Chief Handyman and Fix-it-man. Our sons, now grown men, still come around to help Mom out in a pinch, for which I'm grateful.

A good deal of the attraction to this line of work comes from the dogs themselves, each one with its own unique personality, likes and dislikes, good points and bad. They depend on me and I depend on them. You might say we have a working relationship. But I find that the most fascinating aspect of this business is the people I meet, the people who I talk to on the phone who think they want a puppy and those who come out to our place and know they want a puppy.

Dogs and puppies seem to bring out the very best in people, and I have been privileged to see it happen time after time. What is the magnetic draw a person feels toward a particular pup that has been overlooked by someone else? That unexplainable bond is a mystery that cannot be seen, only felt.

We have had many pups born here throughout the years, but each birth still seems like the first one to me, each one a glorious miracle!

My vet's assistant told me years ago when I first contemplated breeding dogs, "Susan, you will either love it to death or hate it to pieces. You will either want to do it again and again, or you will almost go out of your mind with all the work." And she was absolutely right.

There was, is, and always will be, a lot of time and work involved. But as the wise old saying goes, 'When you love what you do, it really isn't work." Really.

Chapter 2

"How do I choose a pup?" If I had a dollar for every time I've been asked that question over the years, I'd be a wealthy person today. It's the question I am asked most often by prospective buyers. Some people come to look at a litter of pups loaded down with a wealth of information from books and magazines that expound on the personality and basic nature of the Labrador Retriever breed. Many people tell me of the extensive research they have done over the past days, weeks, months, and sometimes even years before coming out to my place. They read books, log onto the Internet, visit pet stores, and talk to friends to get their ideas and opinions. They want to make an intelligent, informed decision, and that's all well and good. The more you know, the better choices you'll make, right?

I have had more than one person show up at my front door with a checklist of items in hand as they examine the pups. Do you pick the pup that runs straight for you, or do you opt for the quiet, loner type? Some people will not even consider a pup who sits in the corner and passively watches the others play. Other buyers will *only* consider the quiet guy. Likewise, some people will not glance twice at the pup that runs circles around them, tail wagging a mile a minute and tongue hanging out. Others will *only* show interest in the lively ones, the ones with a little life in them. Some people are won over by the pup that makes serious eye contact with them while others will opt for the one that likes its belly scratched. Decisions, decisions!

So what is the real way, the intelligent way, to pick out a pup? How do you go about the serious business of choosing a friend for life? Is there a right way?

As I have told my customers over the years, "It's twenty percent in the breeding and eighty percent in the training," and I still firmly believe it. You can have a gorgeous dog with impeccable bloodlines, but if it's not been properly trained, it's actually worth very little. No one appreciates a jumping, headstrong, uncontrollable dog no matter what the pedigree says.

On the other hand, you can have a mutt that is trained to perfection and that dog is a joy to own and is truly valuable.

What will my pup look like? That is another question I am often asked. An excellent indication of what a pup will look like and to a certain degree, even act like, is dictated by its parents. "Look at the parents," I tell people. "The apple usually doesn't fall far from the tree. If you like the parents, you'll like the pup."

Over the years, I have come to a few practical conclusions about picking out a pet. One is that it is usually best to start out with a puppy. You can train it your way instead of working with an older dog who may have ingrained bad habits. There is some truth to the old saying, "You can't teach an old dog new tricks." Don't get me wrong, you can, but it's not always easy. And most important of all, as I told a twelve-year old boy who was debating between two playful pups, "You simply pick the one that tugs at your heart, the one that gives you that special, warm, fuzzy feeling, the one that somehow connects with you." You might not be able to explain your reasoning for picking a specific pup to anyone, but as all true dog lovers know and understand, you'll just know.

In other words, you pick the one you suddenly but unmistakably realize you can't live without. The rest will come. A good dose of firm and consistent training, ample time, and a lot of love will go a long way.

Chapter 3

Dog breeders often help each other out. If someone needs a pup of a particular sex or color and I don't have one available, I refer them to some reputable fellow breeders whom I have gotten to know and trust over the years. They do the same for me. We will also co-operate if someone is looking for a stud with certain characteristics or a specific lineage. One snowy, icy Saturday morning in mid- February, I received an unexpected phone call from Eva Sanders. Eva could make me very nervous, very fast. She was an area breeder well known in the Eastern show-dog circuit who prided herself on raising exacting dogs with only English champion bloodlines and impeccable backgrounds. She bred for a certain look, a certain posture, a certain height, and, of course, a certain price.

My dealings with her had been few and far between because I always felt awkward around her and considered myself outclassed. She knew all there was to know about the proper show Lab and wasn't afraid to let you know that she knew. Our paths seldom crossed and that was fine with me. I had been crushed by Eva a couple of years earlier when she had stopped by one day to look at a litter of pups from one of my favorite females. Personally, I thought they were the nicest, most correct pups I had ever produced.

"Well, they are quite nice," she had grudgingly admitted in her clipped, precise Bostonian accented voice, "although the tail set is a tiny bit high on a few of them and the jaw lines are not quite as square as they should be." She eyed them narrowly as she pointed out further faults. "The noses tend to be a trifle light in color, not as dark as they could be."

I had bred and sold many more puppies than Eva had ever thought of, but in spite of my years of experience, she was the one person who could reduce me to believing I really knew nothing about raising dogs. Around her I always felt like just another novice backyard breeder.

Even her presence was intimidating. She was a large woman whose jet black hair never had a strand out of place. She usually wore a distant, aloof expression on her handsome chiseled face, and her steely eyes looked as if they could bore right through a person.

So I was surprised when I answered the phone that cold morning and heard Eva's unmistakable refined voice. "Sue," she sighed heavily, "I have some customers here at the house who want a pup, but can't seem to find what they want out of my lit-ter." Her voice reflected astonishment, that she found this rather hard to believe herself. "I was wondering, well I was wondering if you happen to have any pups they could look at." She sighed again. "Actually, I'm not at all sure what they do want," she said in a low voice.

I was thinking fast and nodding to myself. "Sure, Eva, I have a few pups left," I said, anxiously biting my nails. I had a litter of eight blacks and chocolates that were ready to go. In fact, I had just started to advertise them in the local paper.

"Well," the cultured voice continued, "I'll send them over. They do seem to have a rather definite kind of pup in mind though." Her voice lingered over the word "definite," and I won-dered about it. "I do hope the roads aren't too icy for them. It is rather bad out today, isn't it?" she ended on a disappointed note.

I replaced the receiver and sat for a moment, thinking. What kind of people could these be, unable to find what they wanted at Eva's, with her gorgeous, perfect dogs? They must be terribly fussy, I decided apprehensively.

My mind drew a mental picture of our barn with its packed dirt floors and gray weathered siding. It was completely ade-quate but far from impressive. I suddenly knew I had work to do. Eva's place was no more than twenty miles away, so there was no time to waste.

"Rick!" I yelled to my husband of over twenty years who was still lounging in the bedroom, enjoying a day off from the rigorous work of being a commercial carpenter in the big city twenty miles away. "I'm running out to the barn to clean the pups' room. Eva Sanders is sending some people over to take a look at them. Could you please tidy up the living room in case they end up coming in?" I added hopefully. And I was out the door!

As I had anticipated, the puppy room was a complete disaster. Eight seven-week-old puppies make quite a mess overnight, and I hadn't been out to do my morning chores yet. I hastily rolled up the sodden, smelly newspapers I used to line the floor and spread clean ones in the hope that the unmistakable odor would dissipate in the chilly air before the lookers came.

I had barely finished when Rick yelled loudly from the front porch, "Sue, those people just called, and they're lost." My face sagged with disappointment. "They took a wrong turn somewhere," he went on. "You know how some of these roads are."

I nodded. I knew indeed. In this part of New England, there were no proper square miles, only a lot of curving, twisting roads. If you missed a turn, you couldn't just take the next road and expect to circle around and end up anywhere close to your destination. You had no choice but to turn around...and some people didn't.

"I gave them some new directions, they should be here in about ten minutes," he added.

"Well, I'm about done in here," I hollered back. "I just have to feed them."

I measured out the puppy food, filled the water dishes and waited. Thirty minutes passed and no visitors. I glanced out the barn door and caught a glimpse of Rick bundled up in his winter coat and hat, tramping through the snow towards me.

"They just called again," he informed me, shaking his head. "They're still lost, this time on Hare Road." Hare Road was five miles away. "I told them to stay put," he continued, stamping his feet on the frozen ground. "I'll find them. I'm going after them with the Jeep and they can follow me back." His breath showed as a steamy cloud as he spoke.

"Be careful," I warned. "It's slippery out there." He waved my worries away and was off, our old dependable '72 blue Jeep chugging down the winding driveway.

I slowly walked back to the puppy room. *What a morning to be out looking at puppies,* I thought. It must be twenty degrees out and the roads were a mess after last night's storm. But I understood. *When you want something badly, you want it now, not tomorrow or the next day*, I reminded myself. I am not a patient person by nature so I completely understand that logic.

I opened the puppy room door and watched the eight puppies chasing each other around the six-by-eight-foot heated room. Tails and ears were fair game for these rascals to bite and chew.

I kept one wary eye on the floor. At this stage of life, all pups did was eat and mess, mostly the latter it seemed.

It wasn't long until I heard the familiar, comfortable chugging of our faithful Jeep, and I poked my head out for a look. Sure enough, there was the Jeep with another car cautiously following. They came to a skidding stop in front of the barn and I watched a well-dressed, middle-aged woman and a young boy step out of the car. Rick helped them down the snowy path to the barn where I opened the heavy sliding door. They came inside, out of the wind, and stamped their snowy feet on the frozen ground.

"Well," I said heartily in my most welcoming voice as I turned toward the newcomers, "I'm glad you finally made it safe and sound."

The woman stared back impassively, a no-nonsense look in her eyes. I could tell at once that she knew exactly what she wanted and was quite used to getting it, even if Eva hadn't been able to figure it out. The boy stood quietly behind her, content, it seemed, to remain in his mother's shadow as long as he could.

Turning to the woman, I said in my most business-like manner, "So I hear you're looking for a pup. Do you have anything particular in mind, like a male or a female, chocolate, black...?"

"Yes, we *do* want a pup," the woman said in her strong, authoritative voice, and then she hesitated for a moment.

I started to open the door to the puppy room as she continued, "Actually, it's my son Robbie who wants the dog," she admitted loudly, turning abruptly towards her son.

I shifted my gaze to the slight boy standing off to one side. He looked about twelve or thirteen and seemed to be shy, although he had an earnest, expectant look on his thin, narrow face.

"Well, that's nice," I said as I turned towards Robbie and smiled encouragingly. "What color do you like best, Robbie? Do you know if you want a boy or a girl?"

Robbie wavered a bit as he avoided my gaze. "I really, I really don't know," he answered in a quiet, serious voice.

His mother cut in forcefully. "It just has to be the right dog! We really don't care about color or anything like that. It just has to be the right one," she repeated. "We had a feeling that today would be a good day to pick out a puppy. I hadn't counted on this weather though," she confessed as her eyes went to the side window through which we could see swirling flakes of snow.

"Robbie's been wanting one for a while, but we haven't had any luck yet," she said as she shook her head tiredly.

Hoping to help matters along, I said, "Well, I'll take the pups out of their room and let them run around on the barn floor so you can see a bit of their personalities. Maybe that will help."

I wondered to myself though. *Most people know exactly what they want as far as color or gender* at least. It narrows the choices down considerably and usually makes the selection process a bit easier and quicker.

Robbie didn't say a word as I started gathering the squirming pups in my arms and depositing them on the cold floor. He just stood off to one side with that searching, questioning look still on his small face. It was as if he were looking for something...something very specific, perhaps something only he understood. The three of us stood there for a minute watching the pups sniff and chase each other around. I knew we were waiting for something, but what? So we waited.

I could sense that Robbie's mother wanted the decision to be her son's despite her assertive nature, so I held up one puppy after another, trying to get Robbie to show me what was going on in his mind.

What sort of puppy is he looking for? I wondered.

He still hadn't spoken. His anxious eyes continued darting from one pup to the next, as if looking for a certain something.

All of a sudden, the smallest puppy in the litter, a shiny-nosed black male, left the rest of his cavorting siblings and ambled straight over to Robbie and looked around curiously. Then he lowered his small head and sniffed Robbie's shoes. He tentatively placed a small black paw up on Robbie's blue-jeaned leg and resolutely lifted his head to look up at Robbie with an entreating look in his small bright eyes.

I looked at Robbie and then at his mother. They were both staring at the pup, staring at it as if they had never seen a puppy before. I suddenly realized that something very special was happening, and I was fortunate enough to be a part of it. Time seemed to stand still for us all at that moment.

Suddenly the silence was broken. "That's the one!" Robbie's mother shrieked excitedly as she pointed at the pup. "It picked him! The pup picked Robbie!" And indeed it had.

Robbie kneeled down and folded the little guy in his arms, eyes all aglow. "This is the one, Mom. I'm sure it is," he said softly. And so it was.

"Well, I'm glad that's finally settled!" his mother said in her stern voice as she strode toward the barn door, pulling her coat tightly around her.

As we left the barn, I congratulated myself. This was one of the fastest sales I had ever made. Then I reconsidered. Had I really sold that pup? No, I hadn't done a thing, the pup had sold himself. I had witnessed that age-old mysterious, magical bond that forms between a boy and his dog. It is an ancient eternal magic that has always been and always will be.

"You know," Robbie's mother confided to me as we walked up to the house to take care of the necessary paperwork, "that other lady, that other breeder, kept telling us how superior her dogs were and all about their famous bloodlines and all their champion ancestors." She paused for a breath as she stared hard at me. "We don't care about all that fancy stuff. Robbie just wanted a pet, something he could love. We knew we would find it somewhere. It just had to be the right one!"

Chapter 4

One early afternoon in late spring, I answered the phone and a deep male voice asked me the familiar question, "Are you the people that raise Labrador Retrievers?"

"Yes, we're the ones," I assured him, wondering if he was looking for a puppy. I didn't have an ad running at the time, but we sell a fair amount of pups by word of mouth, referrals from former customers, so perhaps this was one.

"Well, you don't know me, but my name is Dick Little," he announced, "and I'm looking for a male to breed with my female, my Daisy," he explained. "I was at the corner gas station this morning and saw a fella getting gas who had a Lab sitting in his truck. I took a chance and asked him if he knew where I could find a good stud for my girl. He told me he bought his dog from you people some time back and that maybe you could help me out," he concluded hopefully.

I thought quickly. "As a matter of fact, we do have a nice yellow male you would be welcome to use," I replied as I smiled to myself. Stud service was easy money and no work at all for the breeder. The stud did all the work—if that's what you called it. Usually a breeding took anywhere from ten to forty-five minutes. We had the best results breeding every other day for a total of two to three times midway through the female's heat cycle when she is the most fertile.

"Daisy's in heat right now," Dick declared. "I'd like to bring her down as soon as possible if that's okay with you."

"That's fine," I answered cautiously. "Just so you know, our breeding fee is generally the price of a pup. And I'll have to check Daisy's papers to make sure she's not related to our guy. Also you need to take her to your vet before you bring her out here and have him run a Brucellosis test on her."

Brucellosis is a sexually transmitted bacterial disease that can cause late-term abortions and stillborn puppies as well as sterility in both males and females. There is no effective treatment or cure. In short, it is every breeder's nightmare, but a simple blood test will show results in twenty-four hours. Most results are negative and I have never seen a positive result, but you can't be too careful in this business.

Two days later, Dick called to report the test was negative as I was quite certain it would be, and I agreed he could bring Daisy down to meet Leaping Lion, our lovable stud. Dick assured me they would leave at once.

Dick and his lovely wife, Mim, opened the car door to let Daisy out. She was a shy, slight, two-year-old yellow girl who had never been bred before. I cautioned Dick that sometimes a first breeding takes a bit longer as everything is new, and the dogs sometimes need a little extra time to get used to one another.

We put Lion and Daisy together in the garage attached to the house. There's a window in the door, so we could keep an eye on things, which we did.

Nothing doing. No interest. Absolutely none.

Lion took one sniff at Daisy and walked away from her disdainfully. And Daisy didn't care. She had that questioning look on her face that asked plainly, "Why am I here? I want to go home *now!*" I watched as she lay down on the cement floor and rested her head on her paws, as oblivious to Lion as he was to her.

I told Dick and Mim they might as well make themselves comfortable and have a seat at the picnic table in the yard. This was looking like it might take a while. Rick joined us and the four of us had an enjoyable visit. Dick, true to his name, was a small man and told us he was recovering from a serious bout with cancer and had just finished the last leg of his chemotherapy and radiation a month ago. He was just beginning to feel good again, and I could see the roots of his dark hair starting to grow back on his nearly bald head. Of course, he hadn't been able to work steadily at his painter's job while undergoing treatment or when he was dealing with the weakness he experienced, and the bills had started to pile up.

His plump, soft-spoken wife watched him speak with concern in her mild, gray eyes. They had a young family of five children and a lot of responsibilities, financial and otherwise. I so wanted this breeding to work for them; in fact, I wanted it more for them than myself. Puppies from their own sweet Daisy would certainly be a welcome bright spot in their lives during this dark time, and the extra money realized from the sale of those pups couldn't come at a better time.

Every five minutes or so, either Rick or myself would discreetly peek through the garage door window hoping to see a "tie," the term breeders use to refer to a successful breeding. Nothing was happening. Lion was lying in one corner of the garage and Daisy in another, totally uninterested in each other. I suggested to Dick and Mim that maybe we had the wrong day. Females are only fertile for about six days of their cycle and a male will sometimes refuse to breed if he can tell that it's too early or too late. A male's nose is a remarkable piece of equipment. With a seemingly nonchalant sniff, he can ascertain whether a female is fertile or not.

I urged them to bring Daisy back in a few days so we could try again. Lion had never refused to mate with a ready female before, so the timing must be off I assured them, and myself.

Two days later, the Littles came back with a reluctant Daisy in tow. The dogs went back into the garage once more, with the same results as before, which were no results. Daisy lay in her corner and Lion lay in his. I tried not to act discouraged as I encouraged Dick to bring Daisy back in a couple of days for another try. They were still hopeful about getting those puppies, those future bright spots that could make such a difference in their lives.

Two days later, we once again tried in vain. We were getting to know Dick and Mim fairly well by this time. We sat at our regular places around the picnic table hoping that today would be the day, but to no avail. When I looked through the window, Daisy was whining to get out of the garage and Lion was looking in the opposite direction, acting bored to death. And there was not a thing that any of us could do about it either.

Well, we shook hands and said we were sorry. Maybe they would like to try again when she came in season in about six months, I suggested. Dick and Mim were sorry too. They had spent a lot of time sitting around our picnic table for nothing. They were sorry because there would be no puppies, and I was sorry about their evident disappointment. I must admit that I was also selfishly sorry for myself because there would be no easy breeding fee forthcoming.

As the weeks went by, we completely forgot Daisy, writing the experience off as an unexplained disappointment. One afternoon, while sweeping out Rick's garage, which doubled as a workshop, I answered the ringing phone.

"Is this Susan?" the highly excited voice on the other end asked.

"Yes, it is," I answered, not recognizing the voice.

"This is Dick Little, and I, uhh, I think I owe you guys some money!" The voice was trembling with some strange emotion.

"What do you mean?" I asked, not understanding at all.

"Daisy started having pups today, and she's just had her eleventh one," he crowed proudly.

"What?" I sputtered. "No way. They can't be from Lion! What color are they?" Pure Labs are always a solid color: yellow, black, or chocolate. As Lion and Daisy were both yellow, any pups would most likely be yellow.

"They're all yellow, solid yellow," Dick said, laughing loudly in my ear.

"I don't believe it!" I said incredulously as I clutched the phone. I was almost shouting by this time. "Nothing ever happened between those two. Nothing ever happened," I repeated, shaking my head. "I know it didn't. I checked them every five minutes. Maybe she was bred by another dog," I argued.

"Not a chance!" Dick assured me. "We never let her out of our sight. She's a house dog, you know. Your dog is the only male she's been with. Oh, hang on, she's pushing again! Here comes another pup!" I could hear an excited commotion on the other end of the phone. I couldn't believe this. Twelve pups? When I called later that evening to see how things were going, I was jubilantly informed that now there were fourteen! Unbelievable!

I was genuinely thrilled for the Littles, but deep down inside, I was harboring a lot of doubt. I just couldn't believe those pups were true Labs. Daisy simply had to have gotten bred by a neighbor's dog or some wandering Romeo. I had to see those pups myself to really believe they were Lion's. I had to know one way or the other. So I called a few weeks later when things had calmed down a bit and asked Dick if we might stop in that evening to see the pups.

As Rick pulled into the Little's driveway and parked, I had some misgivings. What would we find inside? I hoped I wouldn't have to burst their bubble.

We were warmly welcomed into the kitchen by Dick and Mim, both of them beaming broadly. Dick pointed to a corner off the kitchen by the back door, and there they were, a very weary, but proud-looking Daisy, and fourteen beautiful, chubby, solid yellow, furry, miniature spitting images of Lion. I could hardly believe my eyes.

Fourteen was way too many pups for Daisy to nurse at one time, so Dick and Mim and their children took turns feeding the pups in shifts. First seven would nurse, and after they had had their fill, they were taken away and placed in a soft, cushioned basket with an overhead light beaming down on them to keep them warm. Then the remaining seven would be put on to nurse. It was indeed a family affair, and it was easy to see they loved it. All of the pups were filled out and healthy, and while Daisy was one very tired dog at the moment, she was also one very contented looking mother, basking in all the extra fussing, special food, and unlimited attention these puppies garnered her.

All I could do was stand there, shaking my head and grinning as I stared at them.

As we were leaving, Dick vigorously shook both our hands and casually shoved a piece of paper in my hand. It was something I was sure I'd never see. It was a check for the forgotten breeding fee!

Just before we left, I turned and took one last amazed look at Daisy and her happy family and wondered again at the quickest breeding that had to have taken place, and the magnitude of the results.

Chapter 5

Dogs can have some very human-like traits. They are sensitive creatures with distinct likes and dislikes. Their feelings can be easily hurt. They can become jealous and they can, and do, carry grudges for quite some time. They are social animals and make friendships with others of their kind. They are capable of very intense feelings and sometimes show the way they feel in curious ways.

Take our dog, Licorice, for example. She made no attempt to hide her dislike and disdain for my mother-in-law, Irma. Now Irma is a very nice person but she has one minor flaw. She does not especially care for animals; any animals, dogs included. I don't think she has anything specific against my own dogs, but still, they are dogs, and thus they do not merit much attention from her. She is content to simply ignore them...and she does.

Having a daughter-in-law like me who is absolutely crazy about dogs and has a whole pack of them around in the garage, the house, the basement, the barn, and various other places must be a bit disconcerting to her, I'm sure. It must be especially trying for her as we live next door to each other, in fact, only 600 feet apart. She hears all of the daily barking and night howling that takes place and even hears real honest-to-goodness dog fights occasionally when our two studs get around each other. She never complains though. She just goes about her business as if they weren't there.

She and my late father-in-law had an outside dog for a while. Her name was Buffy, a small Collie mix, left behind by their son when he moved into an apartment. Buffy lived outside and was fairly independent and she didn't require a great deal of time and attention. Needless to say, Buffy was more my father-in-law's pet than she was my mother-in-law's.

Now Licorice did not like Buffy for some unknown reason of her own. Every time she saw her, she would run straight at her, tackling and knocking her to the ground, then lunging at her with bared teeth while snarling hatefully. It was a frightening sight.

In the mornings when I would walk my younger sons down our long winding driveway to catch the bus, Licorice would trot along beside us. As soon as we neared my in-law's yard, she would race across it, paying no heed to my frantic yelling and hollering as she squatted and did her business on their grass. I'm sure that to her, pooping on Buffy's lawn was the ultimate insult.

She would go through the same routine when I went after the mail at noon and, much to my dismay, once again when I went to meet the boy's bus after school. (She had to be the most "regular" dog around!) In fact, it got so bad that I began to lock her in the garage when I wanted to walk down the driveway. And because Licorice knew that Buffy lived at Irma's house, she made up her mind that she didn't like Irma either.

Since we live so close to one another and because we do get along quite well, Irma often stops by for a quick visit, either by car or, more often, as she is passing our house on one of her daily walks. It's not unusual for us to meet in the open fields in back of our homes on our daily walks; she looking straight ahead and keeping up a brisk steady pace, and me with four or five Labs running around investigating every bush and suspicious clump of grass.

When we meet like this, usually going in opposite directions, Irma does her best to completely ignore the dogs and keep her regular walking pace as we pass.

Now Labs crave attention, and they will do most anything to get it. First one dog and then another will run up to Irma, panting with their long tongues hanging out, all excited to spot her. They give her a few peremptory sniffs and then circle around a bit, pausing for a moment in case she decided to acknowledge or pet them, but she never does. It just isn't her, plain and simple. She concentrates on her walk, and they have come to realize that there most likely won't be any attention forthcoming, so they move on eventually, ignoring her too.

All of our dogs were fine with this scenario and grew to accept it, except for Licorice. She was the old matriarch here and used to all the other dogs' attention and ours too. She seemed to take it as a personal insult when Irma ignored her and refused to make a fuss over her. When Licorice would spot her coming down the path, even from quite a distance away, she would take off at top speed, only to come to a dead stop directly in front of Irma, growling, fur bristling and dark eyes glaring warningly. She looked as though she would relish taking a bite out of my mother-in-law, but it was only a threat. Her main reason for acting like this was to stop Irma in her tracks and force her to acknowledge her. I would always end up calling Licorice back to me and scolding her severely, but it seemed to go in one ear and out the other. The next time we met, the whole act would be repeated. My fond hopes of Licorice and Irma calling a truce seemed impossible.

It all came to a head when Irma stopped in at the house one day. She was standing in the dining room talking to me when Licorice came up and sniffed her casually. Irma continued talking, totally ignoring her, when all of a sudden, Licorice squatted directly in front of her and a huge yellow puddle materialized. I screamed. Licorice walked away as nonchalantly as if she did this kind of thing every day. Irma was shocked. I was appalled. I didn't know what to think. However, one thing I did know for sure, and without the faintest doubt, was that my mother-in-law would never, ever like dogs after this experience. Especially not my dogs and especially not Licorice. Licorice had never had an accident in the house before, but this was not an accident. This was premeditated meanness, cruel and unusual punishment. She had a point to get across and she did. As I banished her to the garage and apologized to Irma for Licorice's strange behavior, I shook my head in disbelief and awe.

Who says that dogs are dumb, that they can't think? I had a problem here with a dog who thought too much!

As you can see, Licorice was an extremely sensitive dog. She seemed able to sense things that people couldn't. One of these times occurred when we brought a seven-week-old puppy home from another breeder in hopes of raising him to be our future stud. I had placed the little guy in a plastic cat carrier for the ride home from the breeders, and he was almost completely hidden from view by the carrier's plastic panels.

When I arrived home and set the carrier holding the pup on the ground, Licorice walked up to it, sniffed it, and growled menacingly. Somehow she can tell he's a stranger, I thought, so I took the nervous pup out of the crate and set him down by my feet. Licorice put her head down next to the cringing pup and took a long intense sniff. To my surprise, she growled again, this time with her fur standing straight up in ridges. The pup cowered in fear. For some odd reason, she did not like this pup. Oh well, I thought; she'll get over it.

But the next morning, as I picked up the pup to take it to the vet for a checkup, Licorice walked over and growled again, ears lying down flat. This was unusual; Licorice loved puppies. Most Labs, especially mother Labs, love pups and will spoil them rotten, letting them do pretty much what they want. But Licorice hadn't even allowed this little guy to get close to her.

I took the pup to the vet and to my surprise, he found that the little fellow had only one testicle. For a pet, that would not be a problem, but for a stud dog—no. I would have to call the breeder as soon as possible and see if I could return him.

As soon as we returned home, I called and explained the problem to the breeder who was willing to take the pup back. He told me he did have one male pup left, but he had someone due any moment who was interested in him. If I hurried and got to his place first, I could simply trade pups.

I jumped into the van with the pup in the back and raced to the breeder's home, about forty-five minutes away. I was lucky and arrived in time and took a look at this last pup. He looked identical in every way to the pup I had just returned. To be on the safe side, the breeder and I both checked the new pup and, thank goodness, he had everything he was supposed to have. I placed the little guy in the carrier and we were off again.

When I got home, Licorice met me and looked expectantly at the carrier when I lifted it out of the van. She sniffed it, and her tail started wagging back and forth like crazy. I opened the carrier door and after an intense sniff, she whined happily, welcoming the lucky fella home. It wasn't long at all before the pup, whom we named Lion, was climbing on Licorice's back, chewing on her ears and long black tail. They were best friends instantly.

Could Licorice have sensed somehow that something was not quite right with that first pup? Part of me says impossible! But why then had she totally rejected it? I really don't know.

When Lion came of age, he and Licorice produced some of our finest pups. Thinking back to the time when we first brought Lion home, I came to the conclusion that her earlier actions may have held a deeper meaning. She may have been, well, just being fussy!

Licorice did have one bad habit that proved to be unbreakable though. She was a wanderer. Whenever our backs were turned, she would be down the driveway and across the road. Sooner or later, I would get a worried call from someone on the next street, wondering if by chance we were missing a black Lab. They didn't want her to be hit by a car they would say, and off I would race, blood boiling, to pick her up. The instant she saw me, she would hang her head in shame and look everywhere but at me. She knew she had been bad, but it seemed she couldn't help herself, for before long she would be off again, and the phone would ring once more. No amount of disciplining or scolding could convince her to stay home and I hated to keep her locked up all the time.

It seemed that Licorice had two friends that lived on the road past ours that she visited the most. One was a German Shepherd and the other was a Husky. Their owners would call and tell me of Licorice's visits, not actually complaining, but worried that she would get killed on the busy road.

The visits came to a stop when Licorice became pregnant and I decided to keep her in the house with me where I could keep a closer eye on her. Besides, she was getting too big and uncomfortable to be traipsing all over the neighborhood in her condition.

Licorice had her pups, and for the first few weeks only left them for five to ten minutes at a time to run outside to the bathroom. As they grew older and needed less of their mother's attention, she quickly reverted to her old habits. One day after I let her outside for a bit of exercise, she disappeared.

"Not again," I sighed as I settled down to wait for the phone to ring. A half hour passed and then an hour. *Where can she be,* I wondered impatiently. *She has puppies to take care of.* Doesn't she remember she's a mother?

Then I happened to glance out of the living room slider window and caught sight of a trio of dogs. Our Licorice was leading the troupe, proudly marching up the driveway flanked on either side by her old friends, the Shepherd and the Husky.

That character, I thought to myself. *She couldn't take her pups out to meet her friends, so she simply brought her friends to see the pups.* And I really do believe that was her intention.

However, the pups were much too young to be exposed to other dogs at this point, so I stepped out onto the deck and called to the two visitors to go home, which they promptly did.

Licorice quietly watched them leave and turned and caught my eye just for a moment. Then she calmly walked down to the barn where she knew her pups were waiting for her. She knew there would always be a next time.

Chapter 6

It was a cool, crisp fall morning in early October, my favorite time of year. To me, fall is a time of slowing down from the frantic pace of summer—a time of taking stock, a time of reflection.

The leaves were starting to change from monotonous greens to brilliant reds, oranges and yellows here in New England. The wind that swept up over our hill from the picturesque Connecticut Valley below had a scent of nostalgic sweetness in it as I walked down the hill to the barn where my ever-present daily chores awaited me.

First, I fed and watered our six adult dogs, which was the easy part. Then I opened the door to our messy and quite smelly puppy room, that held eight rambunctious, but oh-so-precious pups. Whenever the door was opened, all eight would excitedly jump up on the sliding board in place across the lower part of the doorway. That board served a very important purpose. Years before, my handy carpenter husband had come up with the idea of creating a barrier so the pups couldn't all rush out at once onto the barn floor, creating bedlam, every time the door was opened. The board kept the pups in when I wanted them in.

Eight small yellow heads hung over the board looking at me with expectation in their small, bright eyes. Excited yips filled the air that seemed to say, *Let us out, let us out; it's been a long night in here, don't you know!*

I removed the doorway board, and the pups streamed out into the barn, chasing each other's tails and sniffing with wonderment all the shadowy corners only a dusty barn could hold. I sighed as I rolled up the soiled newspapers and laid down clean ones. Next, I changed the water and poured out the puppy food. The pups' sensitive ears easily recognized the sound of breakfast hitting the metal pans and they raced back to their room, each one anxious to get one mouthful more than the others.

I stood there, critically surveying my charges. They were between seven and eight weeks old and, hopefully, would soon be leaving for new homes. I dearly loved them, but by the end of two months, I was usually exhibiting signs of what I call "puppy burn-out syndrome'. They were a lot of fun and a lot of work. I reminded myself that I had them during the best phase of their lives. I got to watch them change from tiny, sleepy balls of fur to chubby, miniature whirlwinds of energy.

Yesterday I had placed my ad in the local paper, so I was hoping the phone would ring off the hook today.

I trudged back up to the house and was just starting to rustle up some breakfast for myself when the phone did ring.

"Hello," I said, wondering who was starting my morning out this early.

"Umm. hello?" a woman's voice questioned tentatively. "Umm, I saw your ad in the paper this morning and was wondering if you have any puppies left?"

"Yes, I have eight beautiful yellow pups," I answered cheerfully. I always said they were beautiful because to me they always were. "I have four males and four females," I added.

"Oh," the woman said softly, and she seemed to breathe a sigh of relief. "I was wondering if we could come out and see them?"

"That would be fine," I answered. "What time is best for you? I'm usually home and can work around most schedules."

That was true and I am grateful I have been able to be home through the years and still earn a bit of an income. Raising animals both necessitates and enables it, depending on your viewpoint.

"Well," the soft voice hesitated a bit. "Maybe I'd better tell you a little bit about myself. I mean us." She stopped for a moment and then continued. "My name is Myra Higgins. The puppy isn't for me; it's for my husband George." She hesitated again. For some reason, the words seemed to be hard for her to get out. The mild voice continued. "George has wanted a yellow female Lab for as long as I can remember. We've been married almost forty years now, and I think it's time for him to get his wish.

"You see, I never wanted a dog. I was too busy raising the kids and keeping up the house; and after the kids left home, I got a part-time job of my own. There just never seemed to be a good time to have a dog," she explained.

Her voice had softened even more, and she was quiet for a moment as if she were thinking of all the years that had flown by. She went on. "George would bring up the idea of a dog from time to time over the years, but I always made excuses. I would say, 'Not now, let's wait a while. Let's wait 'til the kids are gone, and we have more time." She sighed heavily as she continued.

"Well, the kids left and were on their own quite some time ago, and then I said, 'We're both working now, we're too busy. Let's wait until we retire.' Now we're in our sixties and I think he's given up all hope of my ever agreeing to get a puppy. He doesn't even bring it up anymore," she said with a touch of sadness in her voice.

"But you know, I've been thinking," and her voice changed. I could feel the devotion in it as it trembled. "George has been a good husband all these years, and, well, we're not getting any younger," she admitted as her voice trailed off. "I think this is finally the right time," she ended with another sigh.

I was touched, deeply touched. *After all those years,*

I thought to myself. "What a sweet thing to do," I gushed. Then my practical business nature took over once again, and I asked, "When would it be best for both of you to..."

"Oh, it's going to be a surprise," she interrupted hurriedly. "I don't want him to know a thing about it. It's really important that he doesn't know," she repeated. "I want to do this for him, he'll never believe it," she added fervently.

"What a great idea!" I exclaimed enthusiastically. "I agree wholeheartedly. Surprises are fun!" I was starting to get excited myself. "How do you want to work this?" I asked, my mind beginning to fill with ideas.

"Oh, I've got that all thought out," she assured me. "We've been looking around for a while now for a second-hand TV, one that has a big screen on it, you know. I could tell George that I saw your ad in the newspaper for one and that I'd like to take a look at it tonight."

I could tell she had given this a lot of thought. She certainly didn't need any ideas from me.

"That's fine," I said, smiling to myself. This would be fun.

"Now, I don't want you to say anything about dogs when we come to your door," she cautioned. "Could you just play along with the TV bit as long as you can? I want it to be a real surprise!" she begged excitedly.

"I think I could manage that," I said, laughing out loud as I visualized the whole scene in my mind. We talked a bit more, and I gave her directions from the highway. We agreed that six o'clock that evening would work best for both of us.

As six o'clock neared, I made sure the puppies were clean and presentable and impatiently settled down to wait. I positioned myself so I had a good view of the driveway and a few minutes after six, I saw a car slowly move up the driveway. Soon there was a hesitant knock at the backdoor.

Trying my hardest to keep a serious face, I answered the door, my eyes quickly taking in the small, gray-haired, nervous-looking woman and the older, kind-faced man standing protectively behind her.

"Oh," I said, giving them my brightest smile, "you must be the people who called earlier who were interested in our TV."

"Yes, we'd like to take a look at it if we could," the man answered. "My wife here," and he pointed to Myra, who wouldn't allow herself to meet my gaze. "My wife," he repeated fondly, "has been wanting one for quite some time."

"Sure," I managed to say soberly. "Just let me get my coat. The TV is in the barn down below."

I could see the question forming in George's eyes; a TV in the barn? Why is there a television in the barn?

I quickly grabbed my barn coat and the three of us headed out across the yard to the barn.

"It's a nice night, isn't it?" I asked, turning to the couple following close behind me. I was trying desperately to think of something to say to break up the quietness as we walked. Nervous Myra wasn't saying a word, that was for sure. We walked the rest of the way in silence.

As we reached the barn, I said, "Will you wait here just a moment please. Let me open this door," and I slid open the large wooden, sliding door that opens into the main barn area. We stepped in and I could see George looking this way and that, probably wondering where that big TV was hiding.

"Oh, you have Labs!" he exclaimed with a huge smile, his eyes lighting up as he saw our adult dogs in their pens in the rear of the barn.

"Oh, yes. We have a few," I managed to say nonchalantly.

Myra still refused to glance in my direction and she didn't say a word as her husband walked over to the pens and started petting one of our moms.

I gave Myra one last desperate look and motioned to George. "The TV you wanted to see is...is in this room here." I barely managed to squeak the words out as I pointed to the heavy door of the puppy room. Then I opened the door with an exaggerated flourish and turned on the overhead light. Immediately, eight yellow, squirming and excited pups reared up on their hind legs, ears flailing, yipping like crazy, as their heads popped up over the doorway board.

I watched George closely. He looked in disbelief, first at the pups and then at his wife who was hovering in the background.

"George, it's for you," she managed to whisper, and her voice cracked. "I want you to have a puppy."

George was in shock. His mouth hung open and he shook his head from side to side. "I can't believe this," he managed to say as he knelt down on the dirt barn floor and opened his arms wide and eight excited pups jumped into them. He buried his face in their soft fur and turned to me with tears streaming down his face. "I...I just can't believe this!" he whispered again.

Then his eyes met his wife's, and he stood up and went to where she was standing off to the side. There were tears in her eyes as well as he put his arms around her and squeezed her tight. I was not surprised to find I had tears in my own eyes as I walked away. This was their moment, and I realized quite suddenly that I was the outsider.

I busied myself with some make-believe tasks as George applied himself to the very real, very joyful task of selecting his very own puppy. It didn't take long. After only a few minutes he had one picked out, and he proudly showed it off to his tearful but beaming wife. I was surprised at how quickly he had made his decision, but when I thought it over, I really wasn't. George had been waiting for this moment most of his life, some sixty years. He wasn't going to wait any longer.

George walked toward me with one work-hardened hand holding the pup and the other fumbling in his pocket. "How much...?" he started to ask, but before he could finish, little Myra, who was no longer quiet or nervous, bustled over and quickly took over. This was clearly her department.

"I'm taking care of this, dear," she said firmly as she pushed her husband away with a fluttering hand. "This is my present! Now go over there," she directed as she pointed to the far side of the barn. She turned and bent her head towards me as she whispered conspiratorially, "I want to pay you in cash so George won't know how much it is. I've been putting a little away each week for this, you know," she explained with a twinkle in her eye.

As the three of us left the barn together and walked back up to the house, I glanced at George again, caressing a wide-eyed puppy in his arms. He was in a world of his own. He wasn't saying much, he still could hardly believe what had happened. Myra was smiling at him contentedly. She knew she had done the right thing. And I felt what I have felt so many times throughout my years of raising dogs, that I must have the most wonderful job in the world!

After George and Myra left for home with their precious gift, I sat down on the porch steps and smiled to myself as I reflected about the evening and the whole TV story. I hadn't thought to say anything to Myra about it at the time, but it was a bit ironic, I mused. We didn't have a TV anywhere in the house, or the barn for that matter. In fact, in our twenty-two years of marriage, we had never owned a television.

Chapter 7

"Nobody likes Missy," Sharon confessed sadly. "Our dogs are so mean to her." Sharon was an animal lover we had gotten to know through our mutual love of Labs. "I guess I'm just going to have to get rid of her," she continued. "There isn't enough room in this house for three crazy animals. You know the old saying, 'three's a crowd?' Well it sure is! We've got one too many, that's for sure! The other dogs growl at her constantly. They steal food right out of her dish, and chase her around the house. She ends up jumping on all the furniture, just trying to get away from them. It's like a three ring circus!" she exclaimed exasperatedly. Sharon lived in a small house with an equally small yard so I could readily understand her predicament. "I just don't understand why they don't like her," she admitted perplexedly. And to tell the truth, neither did I. Missy was not only a beautiful dog, she was also sweet natured and affectionate with large gentle eyes and didn't have an aggressive bone in her. She never fought back, not even when her food was being attacked by the other dogs. She always ended up giving in and cowering in subjection to her tormentors delight.

"Sue, you wouldn't happen to know of someone who might be interested in buying her do you?" Sharon asked beseechingly. "I just can't put up with this any longer and it's not fair to Missy either." She was right, it wasn't fair. The wheels in my head started to turn, no, not turn, spin. Suddenly, I had a fabulous idea. Maybe I could buy her! She was an adorable dog and only a year old, plus she was completely unrelated to our dogs, which was a big plus in my book. New bloodlines were always welcome. Surely she could be happy at our place with its fenced in acres to run in and our friendly family dogs. The decision was made. I would buy her and give her the good life she deserved. I would rescue her!

So, home Missy came with me and at first, things went well and I believed it would really work. I tried to do everything right. I lavished extra attention on her, trying to make her feel accepted and special. I introduced her very gradually to our pack of dogs and while they weren't openly aggressive to her, neither did they welcome her with open arms. There was no doubt though that she liked them. She had a funny lop-sided grin and a tail that was perpetually wagging. She would try to get close enough to give them a sniff or a nuzzle but to no avail. They were very careful to keep their distance and stood back, snooty and aloof, trying to decide whether she was to be accepted or not. But she was still a happy dog with a wonderfully sweet nature. When I let her out of the field, she stayed in the yard close to the house, never venturing off like some of our other dogs did. She listened attentively and was obedient. She had so many good points that made her so easy to love.

As the days and weeks passed however, I noticed that Missy seemed to be by herself a lot. She would make friendly overtures to the other dogs but they were careful to keep their distance. If she ventured too close, they would growl menacingly, causing her crooked grin to disappear. She would avert her eyes, hang her head, and slink away in disgrace. It will just take time, I assured myself. My dogs are good dogs, they'll accept her in time. But they didn't.

I was going about my routine in the house one day when I heard snarling and yelping outside. Three of our dogs had Missy cornered and she was whimpering pathetically and cowering in fear. I ran outside and quickly reprimanded our crew with sharp words. Missy turned her innocent, thankful eyes at me and wagged her tail happily. It was as if she was saying, 'It wasn't my fault, really. I didn't do anything'...and somehow, I knew that she hadn't. I couldn't exactly put my finger on the problem but I feared that history was starting to repeat itself.

These skirmishes happened more and more to my dismay as the days and weeks went by. Missy was never hurt physically that I could see, but her spirit was surely tried at times. I made it a point to give her extra attention to make up for the ostracism of her peers. I let her come in the house with me which she loved and took her for long walks but ultimately, she had to go back to the barn and field with the other dogs. Days would go by with no altercations.

All would be quiet and calm and I would begin to believe that the war was finally over but then chaos would suddenly erupt and I would be forced to referee and rescue her once again.

I had a hard time dealing with this as our dogs are usually so friendly and have such mild dispositions.

Why then this extreme prejudice towards this loveable little dog? I didn't understand at all .

I had already decided to have Missy bred when she was ready. I thought that perhaps having her own family of puppies would be good for her emotionally. Maybe it would enable her to once again hold her head up and believe that she was just as good as anyone else. And then too, hopefully, the other dogs would respect her when they saw her with her own litter of pups, a queen in her own right. So, I bred her with Lion. He loved her and I was gratified to see that she had at least one admirer. I breathed easier as the weeks passed and she began to fill out. It wouldn't be long and her pups would be arriving. Quietness reigned. *At last*, I thought, *she is finally being accepted for who she is.*

Then one afternoon, two weeks before Missy was due, shrill screaming and snarling emanated from the front field. I looked out the window and saw a mass of furry bodies rolling together on the ground. Screaming for Rick, I ran outside and together we broke up the violent battle.

It was no surprise to either of us that Missy was at the bottom of the pile. She was lying on her back, crying piteously, seemingly unable to move. We could see no blood but she was horribly bruised. She was limp as a rag and moaning weakly as Rick cradled her in his arms and carried her into the house. She tried to stand but collapsed in a heap and we placed her on a rug in the dining room where she lay motionless for two days. I actually feared for her life and checked her every few hours to make sure she was still breathing. For an entire week, she lay on that rug and moaned and slept, and slept and moaned. Food held no interest for her no matter how I doctored it up. The few times she got up at all were to go outside to the bathroom where she hobbled slowly and painfully like an arthritic old woman. The first time she stood up, I was shocked at her gaunt appearance but I was doubly shocked to see that her belly had disappeared. Before the fight, Missy's belly had started to fill out noticeably as her due date was in just two weeks. Now there was nothing, absolutely nothing there. I gently felt her abdomen trying to feel some firmness, some reassurance that there were indeed pups hiding, but I probed in vain. I could only come to one devastating conclusion; the fierce struggle must have taken the pups lives. I shook my head in stunned disbelief. How could dogs, especially our dogs, be so cruel? *What was there that they so hated about her?*

Days passed. It was now two weeks after the terrible fight and Missy seemed to finally be back to herself. She was eating better and walking almost normally. We kept her in the house with us as we weren't taking any chances of another showdown. Suddenly one morning, she began making a nest in the corner of the room, bunching up the rug she had been lying on. Usually, this was a sure sign of impending labor with our expectant moms but how could it be this time? Perhaps it was just wistful thinking on her part but the odd behavior continued. Then it hit me. She was going to deliver the dead pups. After all, they had to come out some way. Poor Missy. I didn't know if I could bear to watch. My heart went out to her thinking of all she had been through and now this added disappointment. I watched as she labored intensely all day and was with her when the first pup was born. I could scarcely bring myself to look at it but I had to. At first my view was blocked by her intense licking and cleaning of the pup but then I heard a faint whimpering. My imagination surely was taking over, but no...it couldn't be, but it was. The pup was very much alive and already squirming and searching for a nipple. My joy knew no bounds as I knelt by her side and watched her deliver seven more unusually tiny but perfectly formed puppies. Never had I seen a prouder mom. Missy proved to be a natural born mother and fussed over her brood incessantly with tender care, constantly licking and nuzzling them. She had fought and prevailed and was now reaping her just reward.

In my eyes, these pups were nothing short of a miracle but I was puzzled about one thing. Where had she kept them? I certainly couldn't feel or see any evidence of them beforehand. The only explanation I could think of was that perhaps during or after that devastating fight, her body had instinctively drawn them up under her ribcage to protect them from any further possible injury. Perhaps this was natures way of ensuring protection. Whatever it was, it had worked!

After Missy's pups were weaned and sold, we came to the sad conclusion that we could no longer keep her in our breeding program with a good conscience. For some reason which we'll never know or understand, as at her previous home, she brought out the worst in other dogs. It was something we could never pinpoint but nevertheless, it was there. It would not be fair to keep her and subject her to a life of fear with our dogs so we made the very difficult decision to part with her.

We placed Missy with a loving family that had no other dogs. They assured me they would spoil her rotten. She would sleep in their bedroom and have the run of their house and yard. There was no doubt in my mind that she would rule supreme in their home. After many pats and hugs and a few tears on my part and one last endearing lop-sided grin on her part, we said goodbye. I was thankful that she would receive the love and esteem she so deserved but I would truly miss her, my sweet, happy girl. And it is gratifying and heart warming to know that in this day and age, there is still such a thing as a happy ending.

Chapter 8

During my years of raising dogs, sometimes something would happen that would be downright unexplainable. One of those events concerned my husband Rick's favorite hunting dog, his pride and joy, his Trixie. Trixie was the sweetest, most mellow, laidback girl you could ever hope to see, when she was at home. But when she was out in the field, hot on a fresh pheasant scent, she would magically transform into an intense dynamo of concentration and action. She had a one-track mind, and that track was birds.

She was a large-boned dog and had an unusual coat color of dark reddish-yellow, which we breeders refer to as "fox red," almost a Golden Retriever color. She was about five years old at the time and had whelped several fine litters of pups for us in the past and if all went as expected, she would soon be having another one. At that same exact time, we had an ugly problem in our barn, which we were trying our hardest to remedy.

It was in the middle of winter when we realized we had a rat problem in the barn where our dogs were housed. And it was proving to be a very serious, very major problem. Everyone knows that food draws rats, but there was no food lying around the barn. Rick and I had discussed the situation endlessly, but we had no idea what was drawing the disgusting buggers in like an army. There had always been a few mice in the barn. We would spot their droppings on the floor or see evidence of gnawing. Rick would set a few traps and the problem would be solved, but this new development was something else.

I pride myself on my clean and neat barn. All of our dog food is carefully stored in large, heavy plastic bins with tightly fitting lids that snap on and off. Our ever-hungry dogs never left even a small morsel of food sitting in their dishes. It was indeed a mystery.

We seldom caught a glimpse of our nightly intruders, but we did see the unmistakable destructive evidence of their presence. Tunnels. We would see mounds of dirt that had been pushed aside as the rats burrowed under the hard-packed floor. As soon as we spied a tunnel or hole, we immediately filled it in. To our dismay, in a day or two, the tunnels and holes had either been dug out again or new ones had been made to take their place.

We had been setting traps for months with discouraging results. Each day Rick baited them carefully with bits of cheese and peanut butter, but we soon found we not only had sneaky rats, we had smart rats too. Each morning as I went out to do the daily chores, I would warily check the traps. Either they had not been touched, or else the bait had been stolen, leaving the traps still set. How those rats could clean sticky peanut butter off a lightly set metal trap and not be caught always amazed me, but they did it, and they did it often. I knew the dogs would have gladly caught the pesky critters if they were given a chance.

But the rats never ventured out into the cement-floored pens where the dogs were; instead, they would stay just out of reach in the main part of the barn where they would get the dogs barking and making an awful racket in the middle of the night.

I was getting angry and desperate. I visited the local hardware store countless times. I was there so often, in fact, that I was embarrassed to show my face again. I was positive the clerk believed my entire house was simply overrun with rats judging by the quantity of traps I was buying.

Perhaps, I reasoned, *our traps are too old and not sensitive enough to snap at a rat's tiny foot or snuffling nose.* So I bought new ones.

I bought wooden traps, plastic traps, sticky-bottomed traps, and even something called a "rat zapper" that promised to instantly electrocute any rat that crawled inside it to investigate. Poison would probably have taken care of the whole problem, but that was out of the question because I harbored a terrible fear of one of our dogs ingesting it accidentally. Some of the things we used worked intermittently, but nothing seemed to work as well as we needed it to work or as consistently as we would have liked.

Once in a while, we caught a mouse or a small rat, but none of the big, bad rats that we knew were responsible for the destructive tunnels.

Rick's theory was that the ones we were able to catch were most likely the young dumb ones that had not yet learned the cautious ways of their elders, and he was probably right. So the older, wiser ones got older and wiser (and bigger) I presumed. Even though we were not having great results with our efforts, we did keep it up, gratified for the few small ones we managed to catch occasionally.

Well, Trixie was soon due, so I moved her into the birthing room in our basement where all of our moms give birth. It has its own heat control and contains a whelping box which Rick had made for our moms; it is a large wooden box, big enough for the moms to stretch out in and nurse. The sides are just tall enough to prevent pups from crawling over it, and there is a ledge around the inside of the box under which they can crawl and thus be protected from being accidentally sat on and smothered by their mothers.

Our moms love the whelping box when their time is near. It makes them feel secure; they know that they have a nest, a safe place to have their babies. Usually about twelve hours or so before giving birth, the mom will instinctively attempt to make a nest inside the box. I put an old piece of carpet or rug in the bottom of the box sometimes, and they bunch this up in a pile and then sit on top of it like a nervous old mother hen.

Trixie had just started making her nest, and since it was early afternoon, I figured it would be a long night for both of us. I gathered up a blanket and pillow to make myself a makeshift bed next to Trixie. Even though I usually wasn't needed during the births, there was always the chance that I would have to clear an airway or simply help a tired mom clean a pup; and, of course, I always wanted to make sure each pup nursed right away to get that precious first milk, the colostrum. And no matter how many times I witnessed the miracle, each birth still managed to seem like the very first one to me. I wouldn't have wanted to miss these miracles for anything in the world.

It seemed I was right in thinking it would be a long night. It would turn out to be not only a very long night, but also a very strange night.

The first pup made his appearance right around midnight, and two others followed about thirty to sixty minutes apart. All was going as usual with the new pups quietly and contentedly nursing. The first unusual sign I noticed as the fourth pup slid out of the birth canal was the sound, the screaming. Even before his mom was able to properly clean him up, an unearthly, pitiful shrieking was bellowing out of his tiny pink mouth.

This was highly unusual. Usually, the birth process was relatively quiet and calm for both mother and pup. I leaned over to inspect the little guy better, and I suddenly drew back. The yellow male pup had a pointed head and nose with odd narrow claw-like feet. Its tail seemed not quite normal looking, long and too thin, almost whip-like. If I had not seen him being born with my own eyes, I would never have been able to believe this was one of our Trixie's pups. She had always had beautiful pups in the past. It was the weirdest sight. As unbelievable as it sounds, it looked as though the little guy could be half Lab... and half rat.

No! I told myself, *no, this cannot be. This is impossible. Maybe I'm just letting my imagination run away with me, but, no, seeing is believing, isn't it?*

I could hardly bring myself to touch the little guy, but I dutifully put him on to nurse with the other pups.

The unearthly noise stopped for a few minutes while the pup found the nipple and began to nurse, but he soon lost interest in the fat milky nipple and once again started screaming shrilly. I watched him for a long time while very disturbing thoughts swirled through my mind.

After a while, seemingly exhausted, he dropped off to sleep. When he awoke, the wretched screaming began again. Only when he slept was he quiet.

Four more pups were born uneventfully, and I went upstairs to try to get some much needed rest. My body was indeed tired, but my mind was racing, trying to make some sense of what I had just witnessed.

When I awoke a few hours later, the first thing I thought of was "that" pup. I ran downstairs, and there he was, lying next to his mother and siblings, but still wailing pathetically as if he were in terrible pain. I noticed that the sound was not as loud as it had been previously, and I wondered if the little guy was perhaps weakening. I gingerly picked him up and examined him, but could find nothing amiss. I placed him back with his mother, but he turned his head away. I tried pressing his small, pointed mouth around a nipple, but he wasn't interested. This was highly unusual. Most newborn pups nurse incessantly. He still continued to make an uncanny, high-pitched shrieking sound. All of the other pups were doing fine except for this odd fellow.

I tried to get him to nurse throughout the day, but he refused. Trixie's dark eyes were anxious and filled with motherly concern as she nuzzled and licked him firmly with her tongue, but even she could not stop the incessant din.

Without nursing, the pup grew steadily weaker, and by the morning of the second day, he was dead. As I removed the sad little body from the whelping box, I couldn't help but wonder about the whole episode.

Our rat problem in the barn was essentially eliminated the following year when we poured a hard, solid blacktopped floor over the dirt one. We still keep a trap or two perpetually set that catches a stray mouse now and then, but the serious tunnel diggers have moved on, hopefully never to return.

At times, I still think about Trixie's strange pup. There were obvious physical abnormalities visible on the outside, but there must have been internal problems too, which I could not see.

I had many questions for which there seemed to be no answers. Why had the pup exhibited an unusually pointy nose and
head, as well as the odd-looking paws and tail? Why did it
scream almost incessantly and at such an unearthly pitch? And
why wasn't it able to nurse the way it should have? Did Trixie's
milk not agree with it, and if so, why not? I don't know the answers to any of these questions, but they have given me a lot to
think about, and I wonder, yes…sometimes I do still wonder.

Chapter 9

One of the many devices we used with hopes of curtailing the growing rat population in the barn was a newfangled invention, a high-frequency contraption that emitted sound waves so sensitive that the human ear could not detect them. "Only animals can hear them," declared the highly persuasive full color magazine advertisement that had captured my attention. It would rid the area where it was placed of unwanted pests, including *mice and rats!* The sound was supposed to make them flee the area within a certain radius of the electrical units, the advertisement promised.

Hurrah, I thought! *This is exactly what we need.* I had already tried all of the so called "normal" ways to catch the annoying critters; and while we had had some success with a few of them, I was getting increasingly impatient for something that really worked, something that would totally annihilate the buggers. The advertisement sounded too good to be true, and I should have known right then that when something sounds like that, well, it usually is. It seems that some of us always have to learn the hard way and to my dismay, it seems I'm one of those people.

When Rick came home from work that evening, I met him at the door and excitedly read him the ad that had piqued my curiosity. To my surprise (and disappointment) he was not impressed. In fact, he was immediately suspicious.

"How can this thing possibly work?" was his first question. "What will it do to the dogs?" was his second.

I read him the fine print of the ad that stated it was absolutely safe to be used with all pets, including dogs and, in fact, almost any animal. It was indeed an amazing contraption it seemed. In fact, I wondered why I had never heard of it before. Why didn't everyone have one if it worked so well?

Frowning and shaking his head, Rick was still highly skeptical of the whole idea. "How can it possibly work?" he wondered out loud again. His analytical carpenter's mind was trying to make sense of the whole thing. "What causes it to work?"

I didn't have the answers, but I didn't need them. I had faith in this thing. The ad said that this device worked, and that was enough for me. I was desperate and wanted to try it as soon as possible. So I talked my still doubtful, but ever-indulgent husband into letting me place an order. After talking it over, we decided to order three of the wonder units in order to protect the large area we needed to cover. I needed two for the barn, I calculated, and Rick would try one in his garage workshop. The past few years, he had found mouse nests in both the lawn-mower and boat motor that he stored there over the winter. This caused problems in the spring when he tried to start the lawn mower and later in the summer we found ourselves sitting in the middle of Crystal Lake with a boat motor that refused to start. *Might as well take care of that problem too,* I thought.

Two weeks later, the anxiously awaited box was sitting in the mailbox. I quickly tore it open to reveal three small, innocent-looking, round, plastic plug-in units. They almost looked like nightlights.

These harmless looking things are going to put fear into an army of wild rodents? I asked myself. Well, I hoped so; the ad said they would, so they must, I concluded, although for the first time, I was a bit doubtful.

Rick plugged one in his garage and I put the other two in the barn. I couldn't hear anything, but I noticed the dogs ears instantly perked up, their eyes darting around nervously as they looked for the source of the strange sound they were hearing.

Oh, well, they'll get used to it, I told myself, and they did. After a couple of hours, they no longer seemed to notice anything out of the ordinary.

The directions that came with the units stated that it might take a few days for visible results. I had been waiting a long time for something that really worked to take care of this problem and I was more than ready for some results. And surprisingly enough, something did happen.

The next morning, when Rick opened the garage door, a mouse came barreling out as though it were being chased by some menacing, unseen force.

Wow! I thought. *What fantastic results!* And so fast too, it had only been one day! Perhaps there was hope for the barn after all.

But the barn was different. The units didn't make any difference that we could see. Each day I hoped to see evidence that they were working, but we still had the telltale tunnels and the old wooden rattraps occasionally still caught an unwary passerby. And to my surprise and disappointment, after that first eventful day, things pretty well returned to normal in the garage.

We continued to find mouse droppings at times and it wasn't long before we spotted another nest. *Maybe the mice had gotten used to the unnatural sound,* I surmised. But Rick shook his head disgustedly. He wasn't surprised at all. It was just as he had expected. But I felt hurt and betrayed. I had put my faith in this invention and for what?

Maybe it just takes a while for them to really work, I kept telling myself. *It might just take some more time.*

Be patient. So I tried to be patient and the months passed without anything out of the ordinary happening. *Might as well leave them plugged in,* I thought. They didn't seem to be doing any good; however, they weren't doing any harm either, I told myself.

During this time, I had two pregnant dogs; Trixie, who was due to whelp in a week and Meg, who we had just recently bred. They were our big producers. Their litters had always been impressive; Trixie had ten pups and Meg thirteen in their last litters. Although Trixie was due in a week, she didn't seem to fill out the way she had with her previous litter.

Perhaps she just isn't showing as much or she's carrying the pups differently this time, I thought.

And then I found out why she didn't get big; she was only carrying three pups in there. Don't get me wrong; I was happy with three healthy pups, but only three pups? What was going on here? This was a first for her. She always had had nice big litters.

Oh well, there's a first time for everything, I thought.

But I had some tiny, nagging doubts, which grew larger the more I thought about them. *Let's see,* I asked myself, *what has changed in Trixie's life since her last litter? Is there anything new?*

There was only one thing that I could think of, and that was the electronic rat repellant devices. *Perhaps those high frequency sound waves are at fault. It isn't completely natural,* I reminded myself. Then the other side of me argued back, *Don't be silly! What can a little extra sound do? What can it possibly affect or change?*

I didn't pretend to know the answers, so I pushed the doubts into the back of my mind and kept the questionable units plugged in. I felt that Meg's coming litter would prove something one way or the other.

As Meg's time grew nearer, I had an uneasy feeling. I scrutinized her figure daily, noting that while she had filled out some, she wasn't nearly as large as she had been with previous litters either. This would be very interesting.

Unfortunately, I could not be with Meg when her pups were born because we were out of state, but my trusted friend Pat stayed with her and promised to call me right after the birth. The phone call I had been anxiously waiting for finally came, and with it came flooding back all of my old hidden doubts in full force.

"Meg only delivered three pups," Pat told me solemnly.

"Three pups," I repeated. "Three pups when she had thirteen last time?"

I had a lot to think about in the days and weeks ahead. *There has to be a reason this is happening,* I told myself. *There simply has to be.*

I voiced my growing concerns to Rick about the electronic repellants. As adamant as he had been in the beginning about not getting them, he was just as adamant that the units could not possibly be the problem. And he had a valid point. How could a high-pitched sound that the dogs no longer even seemed to notice, adversely affect the dogs in this odd way?

I didn't know, but I was positive that something was responsible for our small litters, and I couldn't think of anything else. If only one of the litters had been small, I would not have thought so much about it, but two?

There was only one way to find out, and since they weren't making any difference in the rat population anyway, I unplugged them and stored them away. I had nothing to lose.

When Trixie and Meg were bred again, I was nervous. Would there be a difference or were we destined for only small litters from here on out? This time they were due to whelp the same week. Even stranger, they both ended up delivering their pups on the same day!

I was in my usual place in the birthing room watching one yellow pup after another being born. I was ecstatic! There were twenty in all, ten from each of them. I smiled to myself. Now this was more like it! This was like old times.

The sound units must have been the guilty culprits! It was hard to believe, but what else could it have been? So, I wrote a letter to the company that sold the units and described in great detail what we had experienced and voiced my suspicions, but of course, I never heard a word back.

The whole experience had given me a lot to think about and I've come to a conclusion. It might not be the correct conclusion, but it is the one that made the most sense to me. That is, when you fool around with Mother Nature and with the way things are supposed to be, even sound waves, you may be inviting complications.

I am convinced that there are reasons why things are the way they are in this world. When we meddle and try to change them, anything is liable to happen. I believe there really is something to that old adage of "leave well enough alone."

As for those newfangled contraptions, I guess they're still sitting somewhere in one of the barn cupboards... but I'm not even exactly sure where.

Chapter 10

"Sue, do you happen to have any puppies left?" asked my good friend Bonnie Larner after morning church services one Sunday. Our children were the same age and we had been friends for years. "Jake wants to find a way to make some money and he thought if he bought a pup from you and bred her when she was older, it would be a good investment for him. And besides," she went on, "we've never had a dog before, and we might as well do it now if we're ever going to."

Bonnie's twelve-year-old son, Jake, had watched Licorice's first litter of puppies change from content, sleepy balls of fur to the noisy, playful imps they now were with much interest. He and his mother were astonished at how easily we seemed to sell the pups and were equally astonished at the prices we commanded.

I had gotten to know Jake pretty well over the years and he was a good kid; a good kid but a typical kid. I had a feeling that he thought this would be an easy way to make a lot of easy money. *Oh well, live and learn*, I thought.

"You can have pick of the litter," I assured Bonnie. I had been getting a flood of calls in response to my first newspaper ad, but I wasn't allowing visitors for another week. It takes a while for a pup's little individual personality to develop and show itself.

One evening a week later, the whole Larner family trouped into our garage where we were housing the ten eight-week-old pups. They watched them closely for a while and tried to decide which one would be the one. Which one would make the best pet? Which one was the cutest? Which one was the calmest? Having the pick of the litter is not as easy as you would think; it can be difficult, especially when you have ten pups from which to choose. There was an awful lot to think about.

One pup seemed to be asking to be considered more than the others though. She worked her way from one person to another until she finally ambled over to Jake and started pulling on his shoelace.

Then suddenly, she looked up at him quite boldly as if to say, *Here I am, pick me!*

Jake pointed down at the little rascal and without any hesitation exclaimed, "I want that one!"

"That one" just happened to be the runt of the litter, a bold-eyed black female.

Not every litter has a runt, which is an unusually small pup that is sometimes only half the size of its siblings. Many times the runt dies soon after birth in spite of heroic measures taken by the breeder. Sometimes it seems that it simply doesn't have the stamina to survive. Like other species in the animal world, the strong survive and the weak fade away. The smallest pup is at a disadvantage from the start and often gets shoved off the nipples by the larger, stronger pups. This happens frequently in large litters where there is fierce competition for feeding stations.

But if a runt survives, it is a testament to its nature. It becomes a go-getter, a little tornado, in short, a fighter. It has to be tough to survive, to bulldoze its way through the larger, stronger pups at feeding time. Sometimes, in fact most of the time, I have found that these traits seem to carry through to its personality as an adult.

The pup that had captured Jake's heart was definitely a survivor. She was rough and tough and routinely knocked around brothers and sisters that were almost twice her size to get what she wanted. In short, from the very beginning, she was used to having her own way.

The Larners had never owned a dog before, so I tried to prepare them, as I do all of my new dog owners, for the usual problems that accompany puppy hood, which include crying at night, chewing, potty training, etc. I tried to impress on Jake how important it was to spend a lot of time training this pup while she was young and not let her get away with anything. I knew from the time she was born that she was instilled with a strong-willed nature and would need an extra firm hand. It is very important for the owner to be the boss in the dog's eyes and to always be in control and not vice versa.

I wasn't worried though. I could see this pup was not only going to be Jake's pet; she was going to be the whole family's pet, and I had a good feeling that they would all work together to make this work.

So Jake proudly took his little furry black ball of energy home with visions of forthcoming dollar bills dancing in his head. He named her Tara, a beautiful, proud, aristocratic name.

Before long I began to hear bits and pieces through the grapevine about Jake's wild dog. It seemed that Tara did indeed have a mind of her own, just as I had thought. She wouldn't mind Jake or his mother or his father or his brother or his sisters, or anyone else for that matter. Her favorite antic was to jump up on anyone she could, covering their clothes with dirt and saliva.

When the Larners had company, Tara made a beeline for any young children and promptly knocked them down, covering them with messy and unappreciated licks. She put scratches in the Larners new wood floor that had only been installed the year before. She chewed up clothing and shoes and anything else she could sink her sharp teeth into. She would sail in like a whirlwind and leave destruction in her wake. In fact, Bonnie told me that she was making it a point to always wear her oldest clothes around the house when Tara was inside because another of her favorite pranks was to jump on a person and grab their clothing. She shredded several of Bonnie's long skirts doing this.

Then the neighbors began to complain. For some reason, Tara preferred using their landscaped lawns as her private outhouse rather than her own. She would also dig holes wherever and whenever the fancy struck her. To put it simply, Tara was becoming, no not becoming, she already was, a royal pain!

I tried to think positive. Things would get better. Things had to get better. This was just a stage and Tara would learn to obey.

She was young yet; she would calm down and mellow with age and proper training. I knew that the Larners were trying.

As time passed, the occasional reports we heard did not improve. Tara was doing exactly what she wanted. She was unmistakably the boss!

I spoke with Bonnie a few times reminding her of how important it was to be firm with her. "Don't let her have her own way," I would remind her, and she would assure me they were trying their hardest and deep down I knew they really were.

Then one Sunday afternoon we were invited to the Larners for supper. It was a hot summer day, and we had a picnic-style lunch out on the back deck. While I was clearing the tables after eating, I heard a wild commotion. Children were screaming and hollering around the side of the house. I walked over to investigate, and there was Tara. She had a rope looped through her collar and fastened to the clothesline wire so she could run back and forth. She was jumping on anyone she could reach and knocking down the smallest kids when they tried to pet her.

The kids quickly learned to keep their distance, and Tara was left alone. She continued to bark in frustration and race back and forth on her run.

I walked back to the house shaking my head as I heard two youngsters talking about that bad dog.

When Tara turned one, she should have started settling down, but she didn't. We kept hearing the same reports as before. Tara was not only a disobedient dog; she was an uncontrollable one as well. Her one good point was that she dearly loved people and the attention they gave her. The problem was that she didn't seem to care if it was good or bad attention that she received.

Guilt began to descend heavily upon me. I had sold the Larners this crazy animal. Bonnie was my friend, and I was starting to feel funny when I was around her. She never said anything to make me feel that way, but I began to wonder if she believed I had taken advantage of their family, stuck them with this uncontrollable dog, grabbed their money and run.

I mulled things over in my mind for weeks and finally came to a decision. I decided a friend like Bonnie was worth keeping. I would do whatever was in my power to rectify the situation. I decided I would offer to buy Tara back for the price they had paid me a year ago. She was one of *my* pups, and I *would* take responsibility for her, although I must admit, I was not looking forward to it.

As I had thought, it didn't take the Larners long to make up their minds when I offered to take Tara back. It was plain to see how relieved they were that I was taking this monster off of their hands. I felt bad for Jake though. He had had some high hopes for this dog, and I knew in his own way he had tried to train her. I knew his bright boyish dream of starting a small business with her and making oodles and oodles of money had died, and somehow I felt responsible.

So one evening, Rick and I drove to the Larners to pick Tara up, and after enthusiastically and boisterously greeting us, she bounced happily and noisily all over the van on the ride home.

We quickly learned that Tara craved attention and if she didn't get it, she barked nonstop. She also chewed things she shouldn't and wouldn't listen. Anyone she saw was fair game for her to jump on and slather with drool. But she was one of *my* pups and I *would* deal with the situation. I had to.

In spite of all her bad points, Tara did have some good ones. She was a happy dog; her tail was always wagging and it was easy to see that she had a very loving and willing nature. She was just showing it in all the wrong ways.

I spent; we all spent, a lot of time working with Tara, with scant results. I tried to stop her jumping with the trainer-tested method of "kneeing," thrusting my knee into her chest as she jumped up. It doesn't hurt the dog, but it's supposed to show the dog that you're the boss.

Tara was a slow learner, but we made a little progress, the keyword here being 'little'.

She was a chubby dog, always hungry and she was continu-ally climbing into the garbage barrel and hauling out disgusting treasures that she dragged around the yard. The word 'hyper' aptly described her.

When Tara was two, we bred her with a handsome yellow male with impeccable bloodlines. I had heard that allowing dogs to have a litter of pups would calm them down and I decided to put it to the test. We certainly had nothing to lose.

Tara had an uneventful pregnancy and presented us with eight beautiful pups. She was a calm and devoted mother, but when the pups were eight weeks old and began to leave, back came her boundless energy. Hyper Tara had returned.

At this point, I simply gave up, believing there was no hope for her. She was just a wild throwback to some nameless, headstrong ancestor.

Another year passed and we still lived with Tara's frustrating behavior. At times we seemed to see some positive progress. (Either that or we were just getting used to her). We bred her again and once more she had a lovely litter. This time when the pups left, she stayed calmer and was more obedient. I really can't explain what happened. It seemed as if something finally started to click in her brain, as if a light bulb slowly began turning on. Behaviors we had been working on for years finally seemed to make sense to her. She began to comprehend what we wanted and we were at the same time both amazed and thankful.

Today, Tara is eight years old and has simply gotten sweeter and more devoted to us throughout the years, more willing to please. Oh sure, she still has a weakness for a smelly garbage bag and will always be on a perpetual diet. And yes, she still has the urge to jump occasionally, but not on us. She rears up on her hind legs and jumps...in the air, mind you, mouth open and eyes dancing but never touching us. It is comical to see. And talk about smart, she taught herself to open doors using her nose and paws! We had to change the door knobs in the house to remedy that! She listens well and spends some of her time during the day lazily lying on a rug in the dining room, keeping me company and walking calmly, yes calmly, by my side on our daily walks through the neighboring fields.

She is my favorite dog. Perhaps it has something to do with all the extra time and energy I put into her, but she is the smartest and most beautiful dog we own. She has the classic good looks that we try to achieve in our breeding program. Her litters produce our nicest pups in both temperament and looks. Her pups have proved to have calm, intelligent natures and we ended up keeping two of her daughters for our future breeding program. Although she is getting too old to breed any longer, we have had many previous customers call and wonder when our next "Tara" litter would be available. We receive the most fan mail from customers who have purchased one of her pups, citing the pups personality, intelligence and beauty. She has always had large healthy litters and we have made more profit from her than any other dog we own. Tara is a constant reminder to me about the importance of patience and how sometimes good things require a lot of time and effort, but they are well worth the wait. And sometimes, I remind myself, a good investment takes a while to mature.

Chapter 11

My ad had been running in the paper for three weeks. I was down to one chubby black male and I was nervous. My being nervous was nothing new. I was always anxious when it came to selling the last pup. For some reason, the last one always seemed to take a long time to sell. They were usually just as nice as their littermates but people tended to wonder why this one was left, figuring there must be something wrong with it. I always reminded prospective customers of the simple truth that someone has to be last.

Then there was the problem of the pup being black. There are people who are intimidated by a black dog. They think that a black Lab looks more threatening than a yellow or chocolate one. Personally, I am partial to a shiny black Lab. To my mind, they are sleek and beautiful, but people's preconceptions can be difficult, if not impossible, to change.

And finally, there was a problem because this last pup was a male. Males can be more difficult to sell than females. Perhaps it is their future adult size that intimidates. Males are apt to be ten to fifteen pounds heavier than females and if they are not neutered at a fairly young age, they may wander. Then there is the well-known fact that the males have that innate ability to spray the yard, flowers, and trees with perfect marksmanship, and they seem to do this at every available opportunity.

Nevertheless, the male Lab epitomizes the breed as a whole with its classic broad chest and square face. It truly is a majestic dog.

Taking the former concerns into consideration helps to explain why sometimes a black male is a bit harder to sell, especially when he is the last.

I was feeling optimistic, however, when the phone rang and a gravelly voice rasped inquiringly, "Got any pups left?"

"Yes," I answered hopefully. "I have one beautiful black male left."

"Is he big?" was the next question fired at me.

"Well, he's not big yet, but I think he'll be around eighty pounds or so when he's full grown."

"Good, good, I want a big one. How much you want for him?" he questioned sharply.

"Well, I sold his brothers and sisters for $400, so that's his price as well. He comes from champion lines. He's had his first shots, and we have his parents here. I guarantee his health and..."

"Too much!" the gravelly voice interrupted me shortly. "Can't you come down on the price? I'm looking for a good deal."

I desperately wanted to sell this hanger-on pup, this last of the litter, so that I would have some time for myself away from the never-ending job of changing papers and fielding phone calls. But something in me argued that this pup was worth every bit as much as his siblings and perhaps even more because he truly was handsome. And then I had this funny feeling. This guy hadn't asked one question about the pup except price. He wasn't asking about his personality or his parents' dispositions or anything about the pup himself. Those were all important questions in my eyes that a responsible prospective owner usually asked.

"No I can't," I answered in what I hoped sounded like a strong, forceful voice. "He's a fine pup and worth every cent."

But my caller wasn't interested. Here the conversation ended and I figured that was that. *And perhaps just as well,* I consoled myself.

The next morning, the phone rang and to my surprise, it was the gravelly voiced caller from the day before. "Sell that pup yet?" he demanded.

"No, not yet," I countered, wondering what was up.

"Price still the same?" he snapped.

"Yes, it is," I answered. "He's a beautiful dog." End of conversation. Click went the phone.

Well, I thought to myself, *I can be stubborn too. He's sticking to his guns, and so am I.*

And actually, I must admit that I sort of liked having the little guy around. He was in a crate in the dining room at night, and during the day we went for walks and fooled around outside. I usually manage to get attached to the last one because he hangs around the longest.

The next day, the phone rang again, and to my astonishment it was the gravel-voiced man again. *Now what does he want,* I wondered curiously.

"Still got that pup?" he demanded in his raspy, impatient voice.

"Yes I do."

"Well, I've been thinking that I'd like to run down and have a look at him today. Sounds like exactly the one I've been looking for, big and black!" he added with emphasis.

Well, I smiled to myself; *he's not as tough as I thought! The old codger is finally going to give in.*

He was making a two hour drive, so he must be serious about this, I mused. I had some time so I gave the pup a bath, clipped his nails, swabbed his ears, powdered his belly with baby powder to make him smell especially good, and got the paperwork in order for this likely sale.

A while later, I watched a late model car coming up our long driveway. A well-dressed, graying man in his early seventies stepped out and looked me up and down with shrewd, calculating eyes. I walked toward him, carrying the curious pup in my arms. He introduced himself as Mr. Simmons and gave the pup a nonchalant pat. Then he sat down at our picnic table on the lawn and made himself completely at home. I soon found I had an extremely garrulous visitor on my hands. Instead of talking about the pup as I had expected, he told me the story of his life, which according to him had been highly successful. He told me about his businesses and the places he had lived. I listened impatiently, but obligingly, for two hours, wishing he would come to the point soon as I had things to do.

"How much you want for him?" he asked finally, pointing to the pup, happily running around on the lawn by our feet.

I could not believe my ears. He knew the price from our previous phone conversations and I had given him no reason to think I would be willing to lower it. *What was the motive here?* I wondered.

"The price is the same," I answered quietly, but firmly. "I told you on the phone he was $400. He's a good, healthy pup and I guarantee him."

"Oh, he's a nice pup all right," Mr. Simmons grudgingly admitted as he looked away. "In fact, he's exactly what I want. I've looked all over the place at other pups, and none have been as nice as this guy. I just want a deal on him though. I don't want to pay too much," he whined, fixing me with a look that said he was quite used to getting what he wanted.

I was becoming angry, although I tried hard not to show it. This guy was trying to play on my sympathies and it wasn't going to work. His true colors were showing. I could see them quite clearly now. He didn't buy anything unless he got a deal on it first. It wasn't that I was a hard-nosed person that never ever went down on a price either. There had been times in the past when I could sense that the buyer simply didn't have the kind of money I was asking, and I dropped the price when I felt how much he or she loved the pup. But this guy was loaded. After talking with him for two long hours, I didn't have any doubts about that. It was fairly obvious. Also, there didn't seem to be any real attachment to the dog on his part, except for a casual pat. That didn't set well with me. It came down to this: Mr. Simmons was a "deal" guy and he wanted a "deal" dog or he wasn't interested.

"The price is the same," I repeated resolutely.

"Won't come down, huh?" he queried as his sharp eyes probed my face, looking for a possible weakening.

"No," I answered firmly, shaking my head as I turned away. My mind was made up and that was that. I could be stubborn too.

Mr. Simmons shook his head and we said our curt goodbyes. I wished him luck in finding a dog. He assured me he would find one. He would keep looking, he said, for a good deal.

I was disgusted. I had wasted an entire afternoon for nothing. *That's life,* I thought ruefully. *You win some and you lose some. Better days are coming.*

A week later, I had almost managed to put the affair out of my mind when the phone rang and to my surprise and consternation, I heard the familiar voice of Mr. Simmons.

"Hello!" he said triumphantly. "Just wanted you to know I got myself a dog!"

"Oh," I said with as much politeness as I could muster, wondering why he was calling to tell me.

"Yeah, got a good deal on him," he chortled. "Paid only three hundred bucks for him. What do you think about that?"

Of all the nerve, I thought, *to call me up and gloat about the dog he'd gotten for a cheaper price.*

Be nice now, Susan, I told myself.

"Well, it sounds to me like you got a good deal at that. Tell me a little about him."

I really didn't want to hear all the details, but I must admit I was curious. I could tell he was bursting at the seams to tell me his story and I knew he would end up telling me whether I wanted him to or not.

"Yep, paid only three hundred bucks for him!" he crowed happily.

"Well, three hundred is certainly a bargain," I countered, amazed at the price. "How did you manage that?"

"Yep, three hundred, 'cause he's got a slight problem," he added.

My ears perked up. *A problem? What kind of problem,* I wondered. "Why, what's the matter with him?" I asked cautiously.

"Well, he's got a few bare spots on his fur, some mange on him. I guess that's what they call it. He itches a lot but I'm going to fix him up," he said confidently.

"How bad is the mange?" I asked, rolling my eyes.

Mange an ordeal for the owner and no picnic for the dog either. It is a skin disease caused by a mange mite. The mites burrow into the skin, causing itchy skin along with hair thinning and loss. It then progresses to bald spots and the skin can become crusty, forming sores. It is not a pleasant scene. Treatment is usually prolonged and response is generally slow. Cure is usually possible but not always. In severe cases, there is no cure.

"Well, quite a bit of it," he admitted, "but for three hundred dollars, I can fix him up," he added quickly and a bit too confidently.

"I hope so," I answered skeptically, shaking my head in disbelief. "I really do hope so."

I believe that buying a puppy with obvious health problems is crazy, no matter what the price. The old fellow was taking a big chance, and here's the clincher. He was taking a chance not because he had to, but because *the price was right!* He had plenty of money! That was probably a good thing because he would be getting some hefty bills for the veterinarian's services and the medications the pup would need. And there was no way to know if the mange would clear up. I knew it would not be cheap.

"Just thought I'd tell you about my good deal," he said again as he chuckled loudly into my ear.

"Best of luck to you," I answered, as politely as I could, and to myself I silently added, *you'll need it.*

Our conversation soon ended, and I shook my head in disbelief. *Well, it takes all kinds*, I thought.

It was soon after that conversation that I sold my little black pup to a woman with advanced muscular dystrophy—at a reduced price, by the way—who really needed a companion. I could tell that the pup would be filling a void in the woman's life. He was especially needed, and he would be dearly loved. That kind of knowledge is worth a lot to me.

Thinking back over the whole episode, I was reminded of the old saying: sometimes you really *do* get what you pay for.

And, it still amazes me what some people will do for a good deal.

Chapter 12

Over the years, we had heard plenty of horror stories from other dog owners and breeders about problems with love-struck wandering males coming by when their females were in heat. I have heard of walls being climbed and tunnels being dug in order to reach tempting females but we had never experienced any problems, so we were a bit complacent about the whole situation. However, that changed abruptly one day.

We have two outside pens attached to the barn; they are enclosed with woven wire fencing where our dogs are free to run. One pen is for the females and one pen is for the stud.

Unlike some breeders who let their dogs run together freely, I feel more comfortable keeping them separate. I check my girls each week to see if anyone is in heat. If one is, I put that female in the stud's pen where I actually observe the first breeding and can calculate the pups' arrival date with fairly good accuracy, usually about sixty-two days later. I want no surprises.

My good friend Ellen is a poodle breeder, and she had quite a scary experience some years ago. Ellen was a big-time breeder and owned about fifteen dogs. She routinely let her females run together with her stud; and if she happened to notice a breeding, would jot the date down. However, she never knew if the breeding she observed was the first one or the last one. When one of the females began to start putting on some weight, or generally looking pregnant, she would bring her into the house until her pups were born, whenever that might be. Ellen was experienced, and she would usually have a fairly accurate idea of when the pups were due just by examining the mom.

But she never had an exact date, as she didn't always see the dogs actually breeding.

One time in the middle of January, Ellen had several moms that she decided were all due about the same time. Of course, she wasn't positive, but she was fairly confident, and she had always been right in the past.

One morning when she went out to the barn to do her morning chores, she was shocked to find three newborn pups lying on the cold, frozen ground inside the dog pen. Miraculously, the pups were alive. She scooped them up and ran with them to the house where she placed them under a heat lamp. That was the easy part. The hard part, as amazing as it might seem, was finding the mother. Several big, expectant moms had been sniffing and nuzzling the pathetic pups at the time Ellen found them. She had inspected them closely, but to her dismay, they all looked the same: big bellied, hanging milk bags, and very interested in the pups. And initially, she wasn't able to find a trace of blood on any of them, which would have been a dead giveaway.

Finally, she did spot some blood trickling down a leg, and this mom seemed a bit more agitated than the others, so she brought her into the house; and, hurrah, it was indeed the missing mother. She immediately started nursing those bedraggled pups, and amazingly, they all lived. Needless to say, my friend was very lucky.

I did not relish Ellen's experience happening to me so I kept careful breeding records. Although it involved a little more work to keep checking my girls, I insisted on keeping Lion, our stud at the time, separate. I did like the idea of keeping him near the girls, though, so he could keep a general eye on things and warn us if any strays came snooping around—which so far had been extremely rare. And, I never had to worry about Lion. He was a perfect gentleman and wouldn't think of jumping the fence.

One day in early March while routinely checking the females, I discovered that Tara was in heat. I had planned on breeding her to Lion when she was ready, so I watched her like a hawk. One more day, I figured, and she would be ready to breed. That day was a Friday, and Rick and I had things to do in town and were gone most of the day.

When we returned and I stepped out of the car, I heard an unholy ruckus down by the barn, and thinking about my very fertile Tara, I raced down there as fast as my forty-something-year-old legs would carry me. To my astonishment and indignation, there was a strange dog in Lion's pen fighting viciously with him. Jaws were snapping and fur was flying while the girls watched curiously.

The stranger was quite a picture. He looked like he was part Husky and was truly a handsome dog. His bold look and commanding presence exuded youth and virility. His eyes were gleaming and his ears were perked erect. His thick, brindle fur was ruffled and his majestic tail was plumed high with a proud, sweeping curve to it. The fur was an unusual mottled blend of black and brown that reminded me of something or someone, but I couldn't think of what.

I ran over to the pen, hollering and screaming at the top of my lungs, trying to distract the handsome, but unwelcome stranger. Upon seeing me—and hearing me, I suppose—he hesitated for only a second and then fled down to the end of the field and in front of my shocked eyes, easily sailed over the four-foot-high wire fence as if it were no higher than a jump rope.

I tried following him, but I was no match for his gait and speed, and he soon disappeared from my sight. I ran back to poor battle-scarred Lion and found Rick already there, inspecting a bloody gash on his face. I found another minor wound on his leg, but he seemed in pretty good shape overall. His pride had been hurt though, and he whimpered like a lost puppy. I decided then and there that I would keep a closer eye on Tara, although I highly doubted that the intruder would return. I had scared him away, hadn't I? We had never had a problem like this before; it was probably a one-time thing. This shows just how naive I really was.

That evening Rick and I discussed the incident at length. Neither of us recalled seeing the dog before, although we both agreed that there was something definitely familiar about him. We knew most of the dogs in the area, but we couldn't place this one.

There was an old, tired-looking Husky that lived about a mile away, but he was much too old. Sometimes he would be tied to the clothesline in the side yard when we went by, and it always looked as though he was on his last leg. He had a worn-out, downcast look to his face; his ears were flattened, and his limp tail dragged the ground forlornly. In fact, the only thing he did have in common with our intruder was the unusual fur color, that same mottled brown-black-gray color.

During the night it snowed just enough to cover the ground with a fine, white, powdery dusting. I planned on putting Tara and Lion together later in the day as I figured she must be getting close to her time, but first I had a few things to do in the house.

As I went about my work, I was careful to keep an alert eye on the dog pens, which I could see from the house. All of a sudden, I heard excited barking and savage snarling coming from the field below and I dropped everything, racing to the pens without stopping to grab my coat, screaming for Rick, and there, this time right in Tara's pen, was the mystery dog again! His pointed ears were alert, his intent eyes gleamed, and his handsome tail was curled over his back, making a small loop. He was biting and clawing Lion through the fence while Tara stood off to the side, pacing back and forth, eyeing her suitors anxiously and awaiting the outcome.

I ran down to the pen, frantically waving my arms and screaming, trying to make as much racket as I could. And exactly as he had the day before, the instant he spotted me, the dog wasted no time in racing off for the far end of the field where he once again effortlessly leaped the fence with room to spare and disappeared. By the time Rick appeared on the scene, he was gone.

Who in the world does he belong to? I wondered furiously. We couldn't keep putting up with this! What were we going to do?

Rick checked Lion who, thankfully, was unhurt. Then he kneeled down on the snowy ground and frowned as he inspected the large, clear tracks.

"I'm going to follow these and get to the bottom of this, once and for all. All we need now is a bunch of mutts," he muttered.

Without another word or wasting any more time, he strode off across the field. I watched him until he disappeared from sight.

About forty-five minutes later, he was back with a grim look on his stern face.

"Did you find him?" I asked as my eyes anxiously scanned his impassive face.

"Yep," was the terse, unsmiling reply.

"Well, who does he belong to?" I asked impatiently. "Tell me!"

His eyes seemed to bore into mine as he answered.

"Sue, I followed those tracks all the way up over the hill in back of us. They led right to the red house where that old Husky lives," he said in an odd tone of voice.

I was aghast. There was no way. "Rick, that can't be. You know that this dog was a strong, beautiful dog, not that old, bedraggled thing that lives there," I protested.

He shook his head firmly. "It's the same one, Sue. It has to be. It's the only dog they own. And, besides, I could see where the dog got loose. The collar is hanging right there on the rope. He must have slipped out of it. I didn't go into the yard, I just stood on the side of the road."

"Did you see the dog?" I queried.

"No, I didn't," he admitted, "but don't worry, he's the one. I'm going to call the owners right now and tell them they had either better have that dog neutered or else keep him locked up. We can't keep putting up with this."

His face was angry and his blue eyes were hard. He walked into the kitchen, snatched the phone book out of the drawer, found the number he was looking for, and fiercely dialed. My husband was mad and that didn't happen often. I scurried into the safety of our bedroom, but could plainly hear the one-sided conversation that took place.

Without even bothering to introduce himself, I heard Rick coldly ask, "Do you know your dog has twice been down to my place, fighting with my male and trying to breed one of my females in heat? Impossible? No, it's not impossible. How do I know it's your dog? Because I followed his tracks in the snow all the way from my place to your front yard. Your dog is tied up outside? No, I don't think so. You had better take another look. Oh, you can see where the dog slipped his collar. Uh huh. Okay, just make sure this doesn't happen again, Okay? And another thing, I'd advise you to get him neutered if you aren't going to keep him locked up so this doesn't happen again."

Click. End of conversation. I grinned. My husband had never been one to mince words.

It was still almost impossible for me to believe that the old, weary-looking dog I had so often seen in the red house's yard and the majestic creature I had just seen in our pen were one and the same. I considered for a moment. Maybe my memory was playing tricks on me. Perhaps the dog at the red house was better looking than I had remembered. So the next day, I took a drive past the red house. There was a dog tied to a run on the clothesline, but it was only what I had seen before, nothing new, just an old, tired-looking dog with bedraggled, flattened ears and tail hanging straight between his legs. He had none of the vitality or intensely proud demeanor that the dog in the field had, yet Rick had proved beyond a doubt that they were undeniably one and the same, hadn't he?

How can this be? I asked myself.

It was because of this whole affair that Rick decided to strongly reinforce the smaller of the two pens, the pen that Tara had been in, with wire across the top too. We now use this pen

for all of our females in heat. It's usually easier to prevent something unfortunate from happening in the first place than having
to deal with the permanent consequences later.

Some time had elapsed since that near-disastrous situation
and I gave it a good deal of thought. Love is funny, I concluded
at last. It is truly remarkable. Love is not only blind, but it also
brings hope to the weary, gives courage to the faint, puts a spar-
kle in the dull eye, and brings a blush to the pale cheek.

And yes, I had even seen that love can even change appear-
ances. It can bring the proud upswept curl back to an old dog's
drooping tail. It can take away his meek, downcast demeanor
and replace it with a proud, defiant look. It can put a steely glint
back into his eye and a spring in his step. It can even take
droopy ears and make them stand erect once more. Yes, love
can do a lot of things. It can even make an old dog believe that
he's young once again.

Chapter 13

It had been a hot, busy July day. Trixie, my husband's favorite pheasant dog, had whelped eight puppies two months previously, and while some of them had already left with their new owners, three remained to be sold.

I always felt that the very least I could do for new owners was to make sure each pup was clean when it left our place. I lug them all into the basement from the barn in plastic wash baskets where I give each one a warm, sudsy bath in the deep stainless steel sink in my washroom. Under ordinary circumstances, Labs love water of any kind—puddles, brooks, ponds, lakes; you name it. Unfortunately, baths are not included under the heading of ordinary circumstances. Neither the pups nor I look forward to these necessary ablutions. The pups have one basic goal, and that is to get out of that sink by hook or by crook, and my one basic goal is to keep the pups in that sink by all that is in me. I scrub and rinse while trying to keep water out of their droopy ears, which can be prone to ear infections if water becomes trapped inside. The long-eared dog breeds are much more susceptible to ear problems than the short-eared ones because their ears don't allow proper air circulation, while the open or erect ear breeds dry out much better. Bacteria grows in moist, dark areas like a droopy ear. Water sprays in all directions, many a time making me to wonder who gets the wetter—or cleaner—the pup or me?

After drying them off with some discarded house towels, I clip, or rather I try to clip their tiny sharp nails, which are apt to scratch. The pups don't think much of this procedure either as they try to yank their paw out of my grasp while I'm trying to clip just the right amount of nail. Too little and it's still sharp. Too much and the cuticle starts to bleed, the puppy starts to cry, and I go on a guilt trip for the rest of the day. Usually an adult dog or puppy with sufficient outside time will rarely need its nails clipped as they tend to wear down naturally from walking on hard, rough surfaces.

So for the last few days I had been busy talking to customers and getting pups ready to leave, trying to make them look as respectable as possible.

I had just finished powdering up the last pup after its bath— at least it would smell like a rose garden once in its life, I like to think—when the phone rang. Hurriedly, wiping my hands on a damp towel, I made a grab for the receiver, only to hear a voice ask once again if we had any puppies available.

"We have three yellows left," I answered mechanically, "one male and two females."

"Are they ready to go right now?" the woman's voice queried.

"They're all set to go," I assured her, hoping they would come right out.

They must be young, I thought, *there's loud rock music playing in the background. The beat was reverberating in my ear.*

"Umm...how much are they?" she questioned tentatively.

"They're $400, and I do guarantee them, of course. Plus they've had their first shots and been checked by my vet," I added, involuntarily wincing a bit as I remembered that last whopping vet bill.

"Four hundred...umm...just a minute." I could faintly hear her relaying the information to someone in the noisy background. She came back on the phone. "Okay, that should be all right. Could we come out right now and have a look at them?"

"Oh, yes," I said automatically...and a bit thankfully.

We'll have to eat supper fast, I thought to myself. *The customer always comes first though.* I have learned to strike while the iron is hot, while the interest is there. Most people don't appreciate waiting around. We talked a little longer and I gave her directions to our place.

It wasn't long before I saw the car drive in. A young woman about eighteen or nineteen, with large eyes and long, straggly, blonde hair, came to the door with a dark young man about the same age whom she introduced as her boyfriend. They seemed pleasant enough as they followed me down to the barn where they helped me carry the pups out of their room onto the grassy yard where they romped and sniffed the ground for new smells. The couple started whispering and conferring back and forth between themselves about first one pup and then the other.

I usually leave customers alone for a while when they're trying to come to a decision about a pup. It seems to make it easier for them if I'm not hovering over them. They can say what they really think without worrying about my feelings.

But they surprised me. It didn't take them long to come to a decision as they pointed out the little male. "We'd like this one," the girl said, eyeing her boyfriend speculatively. I nodded. She hesitated a moment and then continued, "We just have one problem. It's the...umm...it's the money part," she stammered.

I instinctively frowned. *Oh great,* I thought, *just what I need, someone trying to get me down on the price.* Well, I wasn't going to budge. These pups were worth every penny of the asking price.

"I really can't come down on the..." I started to say, but the girl broke in, her large, dark eyes even wider than they had been before.

"Oh, it's not that we don't have the money," she said hurriedly. "We do...but it's...it's just that it's all in quarters," she blurted out. She looked at me, waiting for my reaction to this unusual announcement.

"What?" I exclaimed, my mouth falling open in disbelief. "You've got to be kidding! You've got $400 in quarters? Where did you get them?"

She wasn't kidding.

"We've been saving them up for the longest time," the boyfriend said. "At the end of every day, we empty our change into a big jug in the corner of the kitchen. It adds up after a while, you know."

"We've been doing this forever," the girl echoed, nodding her head. She looked at me with real concern in her eyes. "Will it be all right? Will you take them?" she asked hopefully, stealing a look at her boyfriend.

I glanced across at my husband who had just walked down from the house to meet our visitors. "What do you think, Rick?" I asked uncertainly as I explained the unusual situation. I would let him decide. In all our years of raising and selling dogs, we had run into some odd situations, but had never had a proposition like this one.

He thought for just a moment. "Well, I suppose it'll be all right," he said slowly, a little doubt lingering in his voice. Then he shrugged his shoulders and grinned conspiratorially. "I suppose we can take those quarters to the bank same as anything else. It's still money, isn't it?"

I smiled. Of course it was. It was still cash; it would be fine. Why had I been uneasy? "We'll hold the pup for you until you bring the quarters over," I offered.

"Oh, we have the money with us. It's all in the backseat," she said hurriedly, pointing to their small car parked in the driveway.

No way, I thought. "I have to see this to believe it," I said as I walked to the car and peered in the back window.

The girl walked over and opened the car door, and there on the backseat were boxes and boxes of rolled quarters, all neatly laid out in rows. "We know how many rolls are in each box," she said proudly as she and her boyfriend took turns carrying the heavy cardboard boxes over and depositing them on the lawn by our feet. The boyfriend counted the boxes and announced with a satisfied expression on his dark, perspiring face, "Well, that should be $400 exactly!"

Rick and I looked down at our heavy treasure and grinned at each other foolishly. *Oh, well,* I thought. *This is what makes life interesting, and it will certainly make a good story to tell in a crowd.*

We talked a bit longer before the happy couple left with their pup and we put the precious cargo into my van, ready to take to the bank in the morning.

A couple of months later I was at my part-time job auditing the books for a local dry cleaner when I laughingly related the story of the quarters to Eric, the owner of the family-run dry cleaners who is also a good friend. I thought it was a great story and it would be sure to get a chuckle out of him.

To my surprise, he didn't laugh. In fact, he didn't even smile. Instead, he suddenly turned and fixed me with an intense, penetrating stare. His brow was furrowed and his face was troubled.

"Sue, exactly when did this happen?" he asked uneasily.

I thought back. It had been hot, in the summer. "About two months ago, Eric. It was...umm... somewhere around the first part of July," I replied, wondering what was causing him to act so queerly.

"How did these people act? Did they seem responsible? Were they kids?" He fired question after question at me, his eyes hard, boring into mine.

"Well, they seemed okay," I said slowly, trying to think back. "They were young though. Why?"

He spoke slowly and forcefully. "Sue, almost exactly two months ago, the first week of July, we were robbed."

My eyes widened questioningly as he continued.

"Someone broke into the coin-operated laundry in the middle of the night and forced the washer and dryer coin boxes open with a hammer. A little over $400 was taken...in quarters," he added meaningfully as he met my eyes.

I turned away, pondering what I had just been told. "No way, Eric," I protested, shaking my head, not wanting to let my mind dwell on this unsettling possibility. "It's just not possible." I pictured the young couple hauling out the boxes of neatly rolled quarters and depositing them on the lawn next to my feet. "Who would pull a robbery just so they could get a dog? Isn't that a bit farfetched?"

"But, Sue, you don't know, you really don't know," he pressed. "The police have no leads either," he added thoughtfully. "And the only possible proof was deposited, right?"

"Yes," I admitted with a heavy sigh, as I remembered how the tellers had laughed when they saw me lugging those cardboard boxes filled with quarters into the bank lobby.

And he was right. I wanted to say I knew. I thought I knew but I really didn't.

"Well, I guess we'll probably never know for sure," he conceded, after giving it some thought. "It is amazing though, about the timing and the amount. Quite a coincidence!"

I had to agree. It was a coincidence surely, but then again you never do know.

Chapter 14

Rick came home from work one afternoon in the middle of winter and announced with a bit of uncertainty in his voice, "Harry wants a dog from our next bunch of pups." "Oh no," I groaned. "Not Harry!"

Harry was a carpenter who worked for the same company as my husband, doing commercial remodeling work. He was a slight, gentle, soft-spoken guy who looked as though he were carrying the weight of the world on his thin, narrow shoulders. A chronic worrier, he wore an eternally uneasy look on his pale, pinched face. His eyes amazed me; they were never still. They always had a perpetually nervous expression in them and they constantly darted from one thing to another. They seemed to be expressing the ever-present question of, "What's going to happen to me next?" In the classic example of looking at life as either a cup half full or half empty, I was quite sure that Harry's cup would be half empty...most definitely.

Rick had been telling me for some time now that Harry had been thinking about getting a Lab, but I hadn't taken it too seriously. Harry had never made a sudden decision in his life. He had never owned a dog before. Now it looked as though he was really ready to take the plunge and that worried me.

I'm always uneasy when we sell a pup to a relative, a good friend or someone we are apt to see often because we're always sure to hear every naughty thing the pup does, including information about bad habits, how much fur it sheds, the exact amounts and kinds of food eaten at mealtimes, and even bowel irregularities. We have found that sometimes ignorance is indeed bliss.

Rick assured Harry that he could have first pick of our next litter, which was due soon, if he wanted. As a rule, prospective customers will almost die for the chance to have first pick. In reality though, they're not doing themselves any favors. Instead, they're letting themselves in for extra frustration and bafflement as they try to select one pup from many, all of whom are actually pretty much the same. I believe the best scenario is when there are no more than three to choose from. The stress level is much lower.

Be that as it may, Harry would have first choice. One cold, cloudy Saturday when the pups were about eight weeks old, Harry and his two young daughters made the hour-long drive for the all-important decision. Harry had a tense look on his thin face. I could tell that this was going to be hard on him. The girls were ten and thirteen and wanted a little girl pup. We had five females and the girls went back and forth with their father about the merits of this one versus the merits of that one. Harry looked apprehensive, but wasn't fussy; his main concern was that the pup be calm, and I couldn't blame him. A hyper pup is no fun for anyone.

The girls finally came to a decision and notified us that they had picked the perfect one and then promptly gave her the queenly name of Sheba. I breathed a sigh of relief; the hard parts were over, the choosing and the naming.

Now for my part. As I did with all new owners, I sat the three of them down at the dining room table and gave them some tips about things that had worked well for me over the past years, instructions on feeding, training, etc. Then it was time for them to leave.

Harry gave Rick and me one last long searching look as the girls carried the pup out to the car. "I just hope this works out," he said doubtfully, shaking his head.

I hope so too, I said to myself, as I knew we were sure to hear about it if it didn't.

I gave Harry a brave smile and tried to reassure him. "Relax, Harry. I'm sure everything will be just fine. Be firm and give the little gal as much time and attention as you can, and you'll have a great pet."

We waved goodbye from the porch, startled to see thick, white flakes falling and swirling in the frigid February air.

Oh, no, I thought to myself, *this is all Harry needs, driving home with a new puppy in the middle of a snowstorm.*

Rick came home from work Monday with some disheartening news. Harry had indeed driven into the snowstorm upon leaving our home. Visibility was virtually nil and he had been forced to creep cautiously along at a snail's pace. Harry's nerves were taut enough by this time and then Sheba had an accident, a stinky accident that is. The girls were complaining, and everyone wanted to get home as fast as possible, but they were forced to crawl slowly along. They ended up getting home an hour later than planned, with the girls holding their noses most of the way. This was not a good beginning for Harry's introduction to the joys of owning a puppy.

It was soon after this that Harry was transferred to a new job at another location, and Rick and he seldom saw each other. As we found out, this was all for the best. Harry's reports, the few times they did see each other, were none too good.

"That pup!" he complained to Rick after catching sight of him one day at a new job site. "She's a handful! She's been messing in her crate, so besides washing the crate out, I have to scrub her too because she walks through it and tracks it all over," he added disgustedly.

Rick advised partitioning off the crate to make it smaller so Sheba would try harder to keep her space clean. This usually worked as no dog likes to sit in a mess, but will sometimes do its job in a corner if there is too much room. Well, that advice seemed to work. One problem was solved, but there would be others.

A couple weeks later, Rick ran into Harry again. "That dog," Harry declared, "she's got the girls scared of her now. She's so hyper, she jumps all the time. Plus, she'll chew anything," he said in an unbelieving tone of voice. "Pencils, shoes..." and here he paused dramatically, "she even chews chair legs! The only thing she's good at is retrieving. She's crazy about playing fetch with her ball so we do a lot of that."

Small comfort. It looked as though Harry had indeed gotten a hyper one, exactly what he had positively not wanted.

Rick encouraged him to give it some time and to take her outside as much as possible in hopes of curbing her high energy. Needless to say, Rick didn't go out of his way to see Harry after this.

A few months later, Rick came home and walked through the kitchen door with a sheepish expression on his face. "I saw Harry today," he said in a low voice.

"Oh, no," I exclaimed, "now what did that dog do?"

"Well, you know that Harry is a golfer, don't you?" he asked.

I nodded. Rick had mentioned before that Harry often went golfing on the weekends. His dream was to someday play professionally.

"Well, it seems he just bought some new, very, very expensive golf shoes a couple days ago. Harry had put them beside the kitchen door after a game, and thought his wife was going to put them away. His wife thought Harry would put them away so they were left on the floor." He hesitated a moment. "The dog chewed one up completely."

What next? I wondered. Something like this would have to happen to someone we knew well, someone Rick would see on and off again for the next twenty years, in short, someone like Harry.

"He did say though," Rick added with an encouraging note in his voice, "that he was really working with her a lot outside and taking her for long runs. He also signed her up for obedience class so that should help. His wife and daughters won't have anything to do with her anymore, so it's all up to him." Poor Harry, I was sure he was getting blamed for this one.

All was quiet for several weeks. Then Rick came home from work one day with some sobering news. Harry and Sheba had gotten kicked out of the obedience class. The instructor told Harry that he should have better control over his dog, and after a few sessions informed him that it would be better not to come anymore. Sheba was just too disruptive. This was the last straw. Harry was now looking for a new home for Sheba. In fact, he was even willing to give her away. She was just too much for him, plain and simple.

Rick still encouraged him to hang in there, to keep up with his own personal training and runs with the dog. "The older a dog gets, the more settled it usually becomes," he reminded him. "Some just take longer than others. She could outgrow her problems yet."

The next time Rick saw Harry, things had amazingly started to turn around. Sheba still had unfathomable amounts of energy, but the jumping was diminishing and she was obeying him fairly well. She lived for her daily runs with Harry, and in spite of himself, Harry was getting attached to his lively girl. She was all his now. He was the only one who showed her any attention. His daughters were too involved in their own lives, which revolved around school and sports, and his wife simply wasn't interested.

Sheba and Harry's favorite pastime was playing ball together, and they played by the hour in the evenings and on weekends. Harry would throw her rubber ball and Sheba would take off after it like lightning. Even when she was panting hard after an hour of the game, she refused to call it quits. She would still bring the ball back and drop it at Harry's feet, imploring him with her big velvet eyes to throw it just once more.

Time passed and Rick and Harry still saw each other occasionally and all reports of Sheba were now fairly positive. She was almost two and had matured into a lively, but mostly obedient pet, and Harry was supremely proud of her. He had invested a good part of himself in this dog, and it had paid off. Now he was enjoying the fruits of his labor.

One afternoon in late summer, Rick, just home from work, stepped out of his truck with a somber expression on his face. I had been working in the yard and met him as he walked towards me.

"What's wrong?" I asked worriedly, glimpsing the sadness in his eyes.

"You aren't going to believe what happened to Harry's dog," he said heavily.

"What?" I asked, wondering if she had reverted to some of her old bad habits.

Rick spoke slowly in measured tones. Harry and Sheba had been playing their usual afternoon game of ball on Saturday when Harry gave the ball an unusually hard toss and it went sailing across the yard and the driveway, and over onto the other side of the road. Sheba, of course, went running after it, oblivious to Harry's frantic shouts to stop. She had a one-track mind, she wanted that ball, and she was determined to get it. A car chanced to be coming up over the hill, driven by a sixteen-year-old neighbor boy who had just gotten his license the week before. He was going too fast, as several neighbors working outside would attest, and saw the dog too late. He couldn't stop, and his car hit Sheba as she was almost to the other side of the road.

The boy stopped and said he was sorry, but then it hadn't all been his fault. She had run out in front of him. Sheba died in Harry's arms on the way to the vet's office. It was an understatement to say that Harry was utterly devastated. He blamed himself over and over for throwing the ball across the road and causing her untimely death, but it was over, the deed was done.

This was life, and bad things sometimes happened in life. All Harry could think about now was getting another dog, something to fill the void in his life and to give him something to love again.

We had a litter of seven yellow pups at the time whose eyes were just beginning to open, and Harry wanted us to pick one out for him. He said he would trust our experience and intuition. After all he had been through with Sheba, I was going to make sure he got the absolute calmest, most laid-back pup in the entire litter. I had a mission. I watched those pups like a hawk, spending extra time with them to see who the mellowest, mildest one was. The winner was a big male who never roughhoused with his siblings. You wouldn't find him biting someone's tail or pulling on someone's ears. He was very friendly, eager to please, and best of all, infinitely calm. This pup would not put

Harry through the misery he had been through with Sheba. This guy would be a breeze. I was sure of it.

Harry came out once again on a Saturday morning, alone this time. This was going to be his dog, his baby. He was in a good mood, but I could still see the pain in his eyes when he talked about Sheba. He would never forget her.

He seemed to like the little guy I had picked out for him. He held him up to his face, and the pup sniffed his ear curiously.

"This guy will make you the perfect pet," I assured him as he got ready to leave. "I've had my eye on him for weeks and he's the calmest one we have. He's a gem," I said, and I meant it.

To my surprise, Harry didn't seem apprehensive at all this time. I guess he figured he had been through the worst with Sheba, so this one had to be easier.

A month passed without hearing a thing from Harry, but we weren't worried. I just knew that the pup had to be doing fine. He had been a special one right from the start. Then one day, Rick came home and announced he had seen Harry at work that day.

"How's our pup doing?" I asked confidently.

Rick cleared his throat and looked away from me. He took his time in answering. "Well, you know, Sue, it's a funny thing. He likes him all right, but..."

"But what?" I cut in as I momentarily held my breath.

"He likes him all right, but he says he doesn't have much life to him, doesn't have much energy. He likes to lie around a lot and..." Rick's voice trailed off.

"What?" I broke in, not believing my ears. "I don't want to hear this! I can't believe it! You know, we just can't make that guy happy no matter what we do!" I exclaimed.

There's just no understanding some people, I thought, as I shook my head in disbelief. "I hope he still wants to keep him," I muttered, rolling my eyes.

"Oh, he'll keep him all right," my husband said with an impish grin on his face. "Harry says he plays a mean game of ball!"

Chapter 15

Sometimes a breeder may have the very best of intentions and yet fail. This is what I was experiencing, and it was proving to be a bitter pill to swallow. It all started when it came time to breed my husband's favorite dog, Trixie. We had purchased our male, Lion, two years before as a pup with grand plans of using him as a future stud. He was a very handsome pale yellow boy with a broad masculine chest and head. He possessed a mild temperament along with an eager willingness to learn.

We were anxious to see what kind of pups he'd produce, so I put him in with Trixie as soon as she came into heat.

We had high hopes for this litter as Trixie was my husband's ace pheasant dog, and Lion was showing promise of being a first-rate duck retriever. Joining those two bloodlines should result in something spectacular, we thought.

However, we did not take something very important into consideration, and that was Trixie's feelings on the matter. We have found that dogs, like people, can have very strong likes and dislikes, and Trixie made it crystal clear that she utterly detested Lion as a mate. As a friend, he was okay, but anything else—absolutely not!

And it wasn't Lion's fault. It wasn't that he didn't try hard enough to romance Trixie. He did. He pranced in crazy circles around her and licked her face passionately while whining sweet nothings into her floppy, golden ears. He tried to nuzzle her, but she definitely wanted no part of that, snapping at him ferociously and glaring menacingly at her would-be suitor.

As he approached her backside, she would growl warningly. Her coarse fur would bristle and she would suddenly whirl around, lunging wildly and actually trying to bite her suitor. We thought she would eventually give in to his charms after a day or two, but she didn't. She held fast; she could be stubborn, and her mind was absolutely made up. She had made her feelings very plain and Lion was not even to be considered.

I was angry and frustrated. Why didn't she like him? They had known each other all of their lives. What could be the problem? Later, after talking with other breeders who had experienced similar problems with their dogs, we found out that their being raised together might be the problem. Trixie was the alpha dog in our pack and she felt no attraction to this young twerp who had grown up beside her.

Rick and I had a problem on our hands because we still wanted pups out of her. We had already wasted several days of her cycle and didn't have much time left. Perhaps she would accept a different male, and we could still get some pups out of her, but we had no time to lose.

We quickly called Marie Calloway, an acquaintance of ours who had been breeding Labs for years. She was honest and reputable, absolute necessities in the breeding business and had some outstanding dogs. We didn't want to just breed Trixie to anyone. We were fussy. We explained our situation to her. Did she have a male we could use that had proven himself by siring previous healthy litters? One that was calm and had the classic good looks that we tried to breed for? The answer to all of these questions was a resounding *yes!*

Marie understood our plight completely and offered to bring her three-year old male, Sir Winston of Bald Mountain, Winston for short, over that very evening.

I was happy for a chance to try again, but I wasn't overly optimistic. I couldn't get the image of Trixie snapping and growling at Lion out of my mind. Maybe she just didn't want to be bred! Maybe she didn't want to be a mother at all!

But I needn't have worried. Trixie absolutely loved Winston and he her. She took one sniff of his creamy coat, and she started dancing around him, wiggling her rear this way and that. She coyly came close to him, and this time, *she* did the nuzzling. Anything he did was a-okay with her. She was in love, and soon we had a tie.

I could scarcely believe this was the same dog that had tried to kill poor Lion the day before. Rick and I were both delighted with Winston's good looks, and Marie brought his impressive pedigree papers with her. He came from a line of fine champions with many aristocratic names in his lineage. These would be some first-rate pups for sure.

Marie brought Winston over once more, two days later, and again the breeding went smoothly. Now we would just have to wait two months for the results.

Trixie's time soon came and she produced ten lovely yellow pups. She proved to be an excellent mother and we were very pleased.

About two weeks after Trixie delivered, Licorice, one of our black moms, had a litter of eight pups sired by Lion. It was hectic for a while, but all the pups were healthy, and I consoled myself with the fact that when they were old enough to sell, it would be springtime, usually one of the best times to be selling pups.

And I was right. The pups from both litters were ready to go, and the phone was ringing steadily. My hard work was paying off.

One warm Saturday, I had several people at the house looking at the pups. I was kept busy carrying pups back and forth from the barn to the front yard where people could interact and play with them. To my delight, one middle-aged couple, named Dave and Marlene Martin, were interested in buying two pups. This was always a bonus and I offered them a lower price than usual to show my appreciation. Dealing with one less customer was worth a lot. Dave was a broad-shouldered, friendly guy, and his wife was bubbly and petite, a real lady, I thought. It was very evident after visiting with them for only a few minutes that they were true dog lovers.

They picked a black female from Licorice's litter and a yellow male from Trixie's. Dave and his wife had no children of their own, so their dogs were their family, and I could tell that these two pups would be treated royally. They soon left, smiling widely, each of them carrying a pup in their arms. They promised to keep in touch and let me know how things went. I smiled to myself as I went back to the barn to bring out yet another pup for someone. It was such a good feeling, knowing you were making someone so happy.

The months rolled by and at Christmas time, I received the usual array of cards and pictures from well-wishing past customers, and I was pleased to see one from the Martins. Marlene had written a short note saying the pups were doing great, and she enclosed some pictures of each of them. The pictures showed them with their chew toys, and I smiled and added them to my brag book, a photo album which was filled with pictures and letters I had received from customers over the years.

The following summer, my orderly life was disrupted when I received a disturbing telephone call from Winston's owner, Marie. It was news that no dog owner or breeder should ever have to hear. Winston had had a seizure. I felt a knot form in the pit of my stomach as she told me the dismal details. Marie had been in the kitchen making supper when she heard a terrific bang in the living room. Wondering what on earth had happened, she ran into the room, only to see Winston lying on his back, legs thrashing, body twitching and frothy foam dripping from his mouth. She had screamed and tried to get the dog to look at her, but his eyes couldn't focus.

It was all over in a matter of minutes and Winston, although a bit weak for a while, was soon back to his old self as if nothing had ever happened. Marie immediately called her vet and after explaining what had happened, the vet asked a frightening question. He asked if epilepsy ran in Winston's family. That is what the seizure she described had sounded like to him, and epilepsy was sometimes hereditary. Now she was scared. Of course it didn't run in his family she protested vehemently. Winston had a wonderful pedigree. It just couldn't be!

Nonetheless, the doctor cautioned Marie to keep a close eye on Winston because it could happen again. Marie was devastated. She knew only too well that you don't breed a dog that has seizures. The last thing a reputable breeder wants to do is to pass those defective genes on to a new generation. There was something else to consider too. Marie worked long hours and Winston was left alone during much of the day, so it was possible that he had suffered a seizure before and she hadn't known.

Marie did a lot of research about canine epilepsy in the next few weeks. She learned that it usually manifested itself at around the age of three. Winston had just turned three that year. All of his symptoms seemed to point in one direction, so after much soul searching, she made the very difficult decision to have her handsome Winston neutered. Although she had only seen the one seizure, that didn't mean that others hadn't occurred before and it was certainly no guarantee that others wouldn't happen in the future. It just wasn't worth the risk of possibly passing this disease on to a new generation.

After doing extensive research into Winston's background and speaking to people who had owned some of his relatives, Marie found that a couple of his ancestors had died very suspicious deaths. Epilepsy could very well have been a factor although no one had pinpointed it at the time. Marie felt terrible that this had happened and suddenly remembered that he had sired a litter for us. She wanted me to know that it possibly might have been passed on to those pups. He had sired numerous litters in the past and, so far, Marie hadn't heard of any of his offspring with the problem. However, none of his pups were three yet either, the seemingly dangerous age.

I had a lot to think about, and I felt sick. I had sold ten puppies sired by Winston in good faith to people who believed in my breeding program and believed in me. Now I felt like I had betrayed them by selling puppies that might be defective. But whose fault was it? It wasn't Marie's. She hadn't known, and it wasn't mine, for I hadn't known either. All I could do was hope that my pups remained healthy.

Two years passed with no problems and then one day my luck ran out as my worst fear was realized. Marlene Martin, who had bought the two puppies from me two summers ago, was on the phone with bad news. Her yellow male, the one sired by Winston, was having seizures, she explained calmly. They had started a few months ago and were now controlled with medication. She wasn't angry; she just wanted me to know.

I explained about Winston and that it seemed as though it could indeed be hereditary. I asked her to keep in touch and that I would like to know if he got worse or if the seizures became uncontrollable.

Well, this is the first one, I told myself gloomily. There were ten pups in that litter. Would I be getting nine more phone calls?

But no more calls came. I decided the Martin pup must have been the only one with the defective gene, and I was thankful for small things.

Then about a year later, the phone rang one afternoon and to my surprise, it was Dave Martin. He was unbelievably upset and justifiably so. "You remember me?" he asked abruptly. "Me and my wife came out three or four years ago and bought two puppies from you. Remember, one of them came down with epilepsy?" His voice was trembling, and I could tell he was very angry.

"Oh, yes, I remember you," I answered cautiously.

Now what, I wondered as a frown stole across my face.

"Well, now the other dog, the female, just had a seizure too," he blurted out.

"What!" I exclaimed, as my eyes stared off into space. "That's impossible!"

"Well, she had one, and we're upset. We paid a lot of money, as you well know, for these dogs, and now they're both on medication and they have to get liver scans every three months, and it's not cheap either," he added hoarsely.

My mind was reeling in disbelief and going a hundred miles an hour, trying to figure this one out. "But your female has completely different parents and bloodlines than the male," I protested. "I don't understand," I said weakly.

"All I know is that she had a seizure, and it was awful. She fell over and lost control of her bowels, and it was awful," he repeated. "And I think you should know about this." He went on, "My vet says that neither one of your dogs should have ever been bred; it must be hereditary."

"But that's not completely true," I argued and tried to explain. "Yes, it is definitely hereditary in your first dog, but with this last one, it's just impossible. We have her parents and grandparents here, and not one of them has ever had a seizure."

"Well, all I know is that she had one," he muttered darkly. We talked a little longer and before hanging up,

I got the name and phone number of his vet. My mind was reeling. What was going on here? The first dog I could understand; its sire had had a seizure. But this second one was a grave concern. Were my own dogs tainted? Were they carrying a defective gene? And the Martin's, they had paid for two healthy dogs and had ended up with two sickly ones for which there was no cure. I knew they loved them just the same, but still....

The very next day I called the Martin's vet's office and talked to the vet assistant who had the most contact with them and their dogs. She verified Dave's story and I explained my part in it. She told me how much those two dogs meant to the Martins.

"They're like their babies," she explained. "They were in tears when those seizures happened." She told me that during her many years of working with animals, she found that sometimes odd things happened, with no real reason or explanation. Coincidences could and would happen from time to time. This did not mean that my dogs were absolutely at fault. This could just be a fluke. I hung up the phone feeling considerably better and decided to do some research of my own.

I looked up epilepsy in my *Veterinarian's Handbook* and drew some interesting conclusions of my own. While it is true that epilepsy can be hereditary, it can also be acquired, meaning that it can happen for no reason at all. It can also occur after an injury to the brain, such as a sharp blow on the head. Some things just cannot be explained. There is not always an answer to the "why and how comes?" of every problem. Time would tell if my own breeding stock was indeed the culprit.

And time did tell. Unfortunately, three more of Winston's pups did come down with epilepsy. Their owners control the disease well with medication and they lead completely normal lives. All of the dogs had been neutered when they were young, so there was no danger of the defective gene being passed on any further.

As for my own three dogs that were involved, Licorice and Trixie have been bred numerous times with no undesirable results in their pups. We continue to use Lion as one of our main studs and, with the exception of the Martin's pup, in over ten years time, there has been no evidence of any of his pups ever having seizures. There is indeed such a thing as coincidence, but that does not make it any better or easier when it happens to you. To the owners of the epileptic Winston pups, I offered either another pup or a complete refund of their purchase price, which is what any reputable breeder would do. They all without exception, opted to keep their pups which were already such a part of their families. I only wish I could do more; that I could restore perfect health to those much loved pups. I knew without a doubt that their owners would devote themselves to the well-being of their dogs for as long as they lived. I was truly grateful that these special pups of mine had people who would continue to love them and care for them no matter what life brought their way.

Chapter 16

By some odd twist of fate, we had an unusual situation on our hands. A decision needed to be made very soon. Three of our dogs were in heat at exactly the same time. Usually they were anywhere from one to three months apart and that worked out well for two reasons. The first being that supply and demand could handle one litter much better than multiple litters flooding the market. The second, having litters spaced apart gave me a much-needed breather. I am the first to admit that I am not Superwoman. I needed the slower, quiet times since raising my human family kept me busy enough, without the dogs and their puppies adding to it.

Now came the sixty-two dollar question: what should I do? Should I take advantage of an unusual situation and breed all three of our moms at once, meaning that we would have three sets of demanding puppies at the same time, or should I hold one or two of them back? I could always skip this heat and try breeding again in six months when they next came into heat.

There was no doubt in my husband's very practical mind about what he would do if it were his decision. He would hold at least one of the moms back, (preferably two) and only breed one. That would be a manageable situation to him and he made his opinion very clear to me.

But it really wasn't his decision. It was mine. I was the dog lady and I wasn't thinking of the birthing or caring for three litters all at the same time. Instead my mind was fixated on selling three litters of pups, the extra cash I would have and all the bills that could be paid.

I was the bill payer in the family. Rick made the money and I spent it one way or another, either by buying what I deemed were necessities or by paying the ever-present bills that accumulated on the desk upstairs. I had been chiseling away at the house mortgage forever it seemed, month by month and year by year. Selling all those pups at once would almost pay it off. What a great feeling it would be to toss that dreadful payment book in the trash once and for all! Actually, I didn't have to think very hard about this one, my mind was made up. I would do it! I would breed all three and hope for lots and lots of pups!

Rick was understandably nervous about the whole situation, and he did have some valid concerns. "Sue," he asked curiously, "how do you think you're going to handle this? One litter almost does you in. How in the world are you going to manage three?" He had a valid point here.

I didn't answer because I didn't know how I would do it...yet. I wasn't thinking about that part yet. My mind only went as far as visualizing the steady stream of cash that would come rolling in and that hateful mortgage finally disappearing forever.

"Another thing," Rick reminded me as his handsome face deepened into a troubled frown, "How do you think you'll be able to sell them all? You know, there are only so many people out there who want Lab puppies. You're going to flood the market! Did you forget that sometimes you have problems getting rid of the last couple pups out of just one litter?" He shook his head in dismay.

Well, he did have a point, I suppose, but the pups had all gone eventually, hadn't they? I would just have to advertise more and be extra patient. Patient...ha! People who know me very well realize quickly that patience is at the extreme bottom of my scant list of virtues. In fact, at times it doesn't exist at all. I think and act quickly, and I like quick results. I didn't let myself dwell on any negative aspects though; I just kept picturing a house that was paid off, that was totally ours with no more bothersome monthly checks to write out. Yes, I smiled, that would be a thing of the past. And we would have a little extra money at the end of each month if there was no more mortgage, enough money to do something really special, perhaps even something fun, I dreamed.

"And another thing," Rick went on in his skeptical voice, "where do you think you're going to put them all?"

That was a good question. I didn't really know myself. It would be springtime, I reasoned, which would be easier than winter. Everything would work out, it always did. I was determined to be optimistic.

So I went ahead and bred all three dogs. Two months and two weeks later, I was looking at twenty-six squirming, mewling pups, clearly overwhelmed. Yes, we had twenty-six puppies born over fourteen days...fourteen very long days. Trixie, Rick's hunting dog, had eleven; Licorice, Trixie's mother and the grand matriarch, had eight, and Sierra, a female we had recently purchased, had seven. I shook my head in weary dismay as I surveyed my tiny charges. What had I been thinking when I bred those dogs?

Saying I was busy was definitely an understatement. I realized very quickly, but much too late of course, that we really were not set up for this kind of volume. For one thing, we didn't have the necessary room. We couldn't put two moms with their pups in the same room as they got so very possessive and feisty after giving birth. I have been told that a mother dog will even kill another's pups if she has the chance. While I sincerely doubted that my sweet girls would stoop that low, this was not the time to find out. If nothing else, putting two mothers together in the same room would be issuing an open invitation to an old-fashioned tooth-and-nail dogfight which was one thing I could do without right now.

So, Trixie and her large litter went into the heated room in the barn. Licorice and her eight pups went to the birthing room in the basement and Sierra and her seven pups moved into our son Kevin's room, which was also in the basement. We had never used his room before but it came down to this: Sierra and her pups had to go somewhere and Kevin's room had some good points. It was relatively out of the way, had its own heat control, and was close to the basement walk-out door which was an advantage when it came to letting Sierra outside.

You might think that it takes a very special teenager to share living quarters with seven noisy pups and their mother; and while I admit that Kevin is a rather special guy, he actually didn't have much choice in the matter. We desperately needed his room, and it happened to be the most dog friendly room we had. I felt bad about it, but there was no other choice. So while he left all his personal effects and clothes in the room, he opted to sleep upstairs with his older brother. I agreed with him there. Sleeping in the same room with eight dogs would be a bit much.

He had grumbled and complained when I had initially broached the matter to him, but I explained that the pups would be in a whelping box; they wouldn't be crawling around on the floor, and I would even spread plastic sheets over the carpet to protect it from Sierra. It would only be for a couple of weeks I promised, until they could all be moved into the barn.

Since he was still upset and I really couldn't blame him, I did something I had never done before. I bribed him. I promised that I would pay him part of the profit from this litter if I allowed Sierra and her brood to stay in his room. That clinched the deal. Money is a wonderful tool in removing obstacles erected by a teenager. He was quite agreeable about the whole situation until the accident happened.

One thing you never want to do with any dog is to suddenly change its diet. If you need to change dog food brands, you try to do it gradually or else diarrhea might develop, and I don't mean mild diarrhea either.

I knew this as we had experienced it before, and yet when Sierra ran out of food, I foolishly fed her another brand that I happened to have on hand instead of running to the store and buying the kind she was used to, as I should have. To tell the truth, I was getting tired of running, tired of feeding, tired of cleaning, tired of thinking ahead, tired of dogs...period.

Within a day of starting the new food, Sierra was struck with diarrhea and it struck with a vengeance. In the middle of the night, Sierra suddenly had the urge to get outside...now! The new food was going through her fast and she began to whine, but there was no one to hear her. She was in the basement and the rest of us were upstairs sleeping soundly. She started to panic and raced around the room, trying to find a way out. When she could hold it no longer, she let loose and messed all over the room, tracking it from one end of the room to the other in her frantic state.

I was appalled when I found the smelly catastrophe in the morning, but Kevin was furious and who could blame him? It would be convenient to blame Sierra, but it wasn't her fault; she couldn't help it.

"Why did you change dog foods when you knew better?" Rick asked me, disbelief showing in his eyes as he looked around the disaster site.

Why? I asked myself. I didn't know. I just hadn't thought; actually I had thought, but I hadn't done anything about it, so now I would have to deal with the consequences. I would have to clean up the room.

Holding my breath, I scrubbed the smelly, blue plastic tarps that lay across the carpet. That was the easy part. The tarps hadn't covered the floor completely and the pale peach carpet underneath the plastic was nasty...and I'm putting it mildly. It was a putrid mess and so stained that no amount of scrubbing could ever clean it completely or get the vile odor out.

Kevin was livid. I had no recourse but to promise that after Sierra and her pups left, we would not only pay him rent for using the room as we had previously agreed, but that we would also get him a new carpet.

For some reason, this whole scenario was not turning out the way I had envisioned it a mere two months ago. In fact, these were turning out to be quite a costly bunch of pups!

All things considered though, I did have a lot to be thankful for. All twenty-six puppies were thriving. I kept a close eye on them and in the beginning, would pull the fat ones off the nipples for a time and put the skinny ones on. I especially had to do this with Trixie's litter of eleven. It was easy for one or two of the smaller ones to be pushed off to the side by some of the heftier ones when there were so many. I was grateful the pups were all healthy and gaining weight, but I did feel as though I was playing musical moms for a while.

First, I would let one mother outside to do her job. After fifteen minutes, I would bring her back in and let out another one. I would call that one back in after about fifteen minutes and then let out the last one for her fifteen minutes. I did this every few hours in the beginning as I had a very real and vivid horror of another accident occurring.

In between times, I watered and fed the moms, who were going through enormous quantities of food in order to provide enough milk for their rapidly growing pups. Some days I could scarcely keep track of who was out, who was in, or who would go out next. It was enough to make your head spin! But I didn't dare complain. After all, this had been my idea, and my husband was not adverse to reminding me every once in a while that it most certainly had not been his.

The weeks passed in a blur and the two batches of pups in the house were now old enough to be moved into the barn. They were eating softened puppy food at this point and only nursed occasionally. There was only one problem. There was only one room in the barn to hold all twenty-six puppies. Somehow I would have to keep the litters separate so their AKC papers would be accurate, which was very important.

Someone had once told me that putting fingernail polish on the pups' toenails would be a good way to tell them apart. That sounded good initially, but it was a fiasco. Trying to put sticky polish on the tiny toenails of twenty-six wiggly, squirmy pups is not an easy feat. And for some reason, the polish wore off way too quickly and didn't show up as well as I needed it to.

What to do? My bright husband was feeling sorry for me and had the ingenious idea of marking the inside of each pup's ear with a permanent marker, a different color for each litter.

This worked fairly well; I just needed to redo the ears every few days as the color wore off from all the ear pulling and biting that went on in a room with twenty-six rambunctious balls of energy in it.

The three mothers were another problem. Even though they were not nursing regularly at this point, they still loved their babies and wanted to be with them some of the time. But the moms could not go in the room together as they were still a bit touchy with each other and possessive of their own pups.

So I did the only thing I could. I simply let each mom take her turn in the noisy room where she was instantly mobbed by twenty-six small bodies. By watching through the window in the door, I could tell when she had enough of the pups and I would open the door so she could escape. The pups couldn't follow her because of a board placed across the bottom part of the door that they could not yet climb over.

Then the next mom would enter and then the next. It was crazy, but it seemed to work for everyone as far as I could tell. The moms were able to satisfy their maternal longings, and the pups were not being cut off cold turkey from their moms and could even nurse if they so desired, and were quick enough, I should add.

The situation was taking its toll on me. I went nowhere; I did nothing but take care of dogs from morning 'til night. Trying to keep twenty-six puppies clean in a fairly small, contained area is a tricky business in itself. I walked up and down our street on garbage pickup day and gathered up the newspapers that the neighbors had put out. I lined the puppy room floor with them twice a day and rolled them up again twice a day to replace them with fresh ones.

And the food we went through! It seemed I was constantly shelling out money for forty-pound bags of puppy food. I was a regular customer at the local bulk food store, that was for sure. Daily, I placed shallow pans of drinking water on the floor for the pups, but they decided the pans were for splashing and swimming. These were Labs, I reminded myself wryly, and Labs love water. Needless to say, the water pans didn't stay full very long, and the papers on the floor continued to be soggy.

Time was marching on, but not as fast as I would have liked. The pups were now old enough to advertise in the newspaper. They weren't ready to actually leave yet, but people could come and pick out the pup they wanted. This involved yet another complete set of ear markings. One color was for litter identification and the other color signified that they were sold. With so many pups to keep track of, my worst fear was that I would inadvertently sell the same puppy twice. I even woke up one morning at 2:00 a.m. in a sweaty panic, sure I had a pup going to the wrong people, but I didn't. I kept careful records of each sale in a spiral notebook which I kept in my bedroom and guarded with my life.

This notebook was invaluably precious, as there was no possible way I could remember which pup was sold and to whom. Once when I mislaid the notebook for a few hours, I was panic stricken. I tore through the house, running from room to room, sifting through piles of magazines and papers, and even recruiting the boys to help look for "Mom's dog book." My joy knew no bounds when it was finally found.

It was springtime, a good time for selling puppies, and I was lucky. My phone rang constantly for which I was grateful, but I was tired of talking, tired of explaining, tired of giving directions, and tired of always being nice to all of these potential customers. In short, I was burned out.

Another week passed. The first pups would be leaving on the coming weekend. There was one more job to be done before then. I had to cart all twenty-six of the rascals to the vet for their first shots and physicals. I like to think of myself as a brave person, but I was not nearly brave enough to lug them all in by myself to the vet's office. I called up my good friend Linda, who is a dog owner and animal lover, and told her I urgently needed her help. I would be happy to treat her to a gourmet lunch at an exquisite little restaurant that had recently opened nearby, I promised. Bribery was no longer a problem for me. "Whatever it took" was my motto now. She laughed and good-naturedly took me up on my offer. Actually, Linda is the type of person who would volunteer her help even if there wasn't a promise of lunch.

What would I ever do without my good friends? I wondered.

So the morning of the appointment, I loaded all the pups up in four wash baskets, and Linda and I rattled off in my old red van that smelled like, well, I won't say what it smelled like, but you can use your imagination.

Of course, two of the baskets tipped over during the seven-mile ride, spilling noisily protesting pups in all directions. I cowardly kept my eyes glued to the road and sent Linda climbing over the seats to straighten things up as best as she could.

When we arrived at the vet's office and started toting the baskets full of wide-eyed, curious pups inside, we got a lot of stares—too many stares. I felt uncomfortable, afraid that people were going to think I was running a puppy mill or something illegal.

My vet and his assistants are super people who are not easily rattled by anything, which I really appreciated this morning. We decided to set up an assembly line to make things move smoother and faster. We would pick up a pup, weigh it, and hand it to the vet. He would then check its heart, ears, mouth, eyes, genitals, belly, etc. Next would come the distemper/parvo vaccine and the oral worm medicine. Then an assistant would take the pup from the vet and clip its sharp nails and fill out the physical exam report on it. Then back into the basket it would go. We did this for two hours straight and when it was all over, I braced myself for the bill, and believe me, it was a whopper.

Oh, well, that's the way it goes. I reminded myself of that old cliché, "You have to spend money to make money," and hoped it was true because I was surely spending.

Finally, the day I had long dreamed about arrived.

It was time for the first pups to leave. Hurrah! However, before they left, each one needed a bath, so Rick and I set to work. We checked the ear colors against my precious notebook and carted the soon-to-be departing pups from the barn into the basement where I soaped and rinsed their small, pudgy bodies.

Then I towel dried them and carried them upstairs where I put them in a large metal crate where they stayed until their owners came for them later in the day.

And when the new owners came, I tried hard to be pleasant. There was always the talking, the counseling, and the encouraging that went along with each departing pup. I was both happy and exhausted, and I stayed that way for four weeks until all of the pups were gone. Yes, it was amazing, but they did all go.

I learned a lesson, I told myself, as the last ones left. *I will never, ever be crazy enough to breed more than two females at a time, and even that will be pushing it.*

I will never, ever again put myself and my family through what we have just been through. What got into me four months ago when I bred these moms? What was I thinking? Where was my head?

I knew the answer. My head had been up in the clouds, dreaming about the lovely money, but now it was firmly back on my shoulders where it belonged.

A month later, my weary twenty-six-puppy memories were starting to recede into the humdrum background of everyday life as I triumphantly paid the final installment on our mortgage. What a feeling!

And then our son, Kevin, who rather sheepishly admitted that he had never particularly liked his pale peach carpet anyway, was rewarded with new, spotlessly clean, sweet-smelling carpet tiles for his room. He had of course, already been paid his rather substantial room rent.

And then something even more wonderful happened. We had the once-in-a-lifetime opportunity to take our whole family and my parents to the Caribbean in February. True, we wouldn't be staying in a fancy high rise hotel. We would be camping in lowly tents so we could afford for everyone to go, but we would still be there on the beach, and most important of all, we would be together.

The extra money realized from all those spring pups would not only make the trip a possibility, it would make it a reality.

I have learned the hard way that opportunity seldom knocks twice, that sometimes you get only one chance at something, so you had best take it when you have that chance. You may never get another. We decided to take it, to splurge and go for it!

Many months later, in the middle of a cold, blustery, New England winter, the six of us boarded a jet for the balmy Caribbean. I was looking forward to meeting my parents there in a matter of hours. True, we were loaded down with tents, a cook stove, sleeping bags, and suitcases full of paper plates, dry cereal, and clothesline, but we were on our way to paradise and nothing else mattered.

A few days later, as I was blissfully floating on my back in the warm, clear, turquoise water with the brilliant sun beaming down upon my warmth-starved body, I had plenty of time to think about a lot of things. I came to the conclusion that it really hadn't been so bad last spring. In fact, if I had the chance, I mused, perhaps I would even consider doing the same thing again. Sure it had taken some time and some hard work, but you know—it really hadn't been so bad after all!

Chapter 17

I t was in the middle of September and our gray pickup truck was loaded from the floorboards to the ceiling. In the morning we were leaving for Michigan, where I had been raised and where my parents and two married brothers lived with their families. Rick planned on helping my oldest brother Don with the addition he was putting on his seventy-year-old home.

It had been a fairly small house when he and his wife, Tina, had bought it several years earlier. It had been a bit tight but adequate with two children, but when a long-awaited and much longed for baby girl had come along rather unexpectedly in the last year, the extra room was needed more than ever.

The thought of taking out another mortgage went against my very practical brother's nature, so he decided that he would build the addition himself to cut costs. He was young, energetic, a quick learner, and above all, he had a good dose of common sense. He decided to take the summer off from his regular job as a machinist so he could devote all of his time to the all-encompassing task—and he had done just that.

He had worked all summer from daybreak to sundown trying to get as much done as possible before he had to return to his regular job in October.

It had been my bright idea to make the trip out. Don was at the sheetrock stage, and Rick, installs countless panels of sheetrock in his job and has the specialized tools for doing that work. Rick's work was a bit slow at the moment, and it just seemed like going out to help was the right thing to do.

We would be taking Curt, our youngest son, with us. Nate, the second youngest, was staying with friends, and the two oldest would be home to manage the house and dogs. Managing the dogs was not a complicated task. It consisted mainly of letting them out in their runs in the morning, and feeding, watering, and locking them back up in the barn at night. It was really very simple except for one major detail, Tara.

Tara, my favorite black mom, was in heat. I watched my girls like a hawk when they were in heat and fertile, and now there would be no one to keep an eye on her. A dog's heat cycle usually lasts about twenty-one days. The fertile period is in the middle of the cycle; and as luck would have it, Tara would be at her most fertile stage the entire time we were gone, and I was adamant that I did not want her bred.

I was burned out from taking care of one litter of puppies after another from the preceding winter, spring, and summer, and I needed a break. Plus, I did not want winter pups, period, which these would be. If she were bred now, the puppies would be born in November, a cold, rainy, sometimes snowy, miserable month here in New England. We would have the pups through December and January, both cold, miserable months, before they would be ready to leave.

It's easy to see that I'm a warm-weather person for some very good reasons. First and foremost, cold weather pups are much more work than warm weather ones. They have to stay in their heated room in the barn the entire time, making it much more work for me to keep them dry and clean than it would be in the summer when they could run around in their breezy outside pen. Then too, it seems my winter pups were always more likely than my warm-weather ones to develop health issues like rashes and ugly pimples on their undersides caused by the damp, raw weather which penetrated our drafty barn. The rashes were sometimes difficult to clear up and often required medication.

Then there was yet another thing to worry about, chilled puppies. Sometimes the heat is a little tricky to control in our drafty barn, and I am always worrying about the pups catching cold. A thoroughly chilled puppy is sometimes nearly impossible to warm up, and very often it does not survive.

I had good valid reasons why I didn't want Tara bred now. We would simply skip this heat and breed her in six months when she came in season again.

We have two large wooden stalls in our barn which we originally built for the llamas we raised about fifteen years ago; but that's another life, another story. Anyway, we now use the cement-floored stalls as dog pens, and each has a large outside run, completely fenced in by my wonderfully handy husband. One of the two pens was smaller than the other, and this I nicknamed the in-heat pen where, as the name suggests, we put our girls when they are in heat. "This pen is impenetrable," I would brag, and I firmly believed it. To separate it from the other pen, there are heavy wooden slats an inch apart that start at the floor and extend up about five feet, where wire mesh fencing takes over and rises to the ceiling. The run outside this special pen is completely enclosed with the same wire mesh. Even the top of the pen is covered with wire to discourage any wandering Romeos who would like to try sailing over the top to do some courting on the sly.

Before we left, I put Tara in the in-heat pen with her sister Meg to keep her company, and Trixie, her other sister, and Freeman, one of our yellow studs, in the other pen. It was impossible for Freeman to get into the in-heat pen without someone actually opening the door and letting him in. I liked the idea of having Freeman close by though, as he would alarm our sons by his barking if any amorous males ventured near.

"Lock the dogs up each night," I reminded Doug and Kevin. "Be careful when you open their doors each morning to feed them so one doesn't slip out," I admonished sternly. "And most of all, whatever you do," I added, "Keep a close eye on Tara. I do *not* want her pregnant!" I declared.

"Not a problem, Mom," they both said reassuringly. "Don't worry about a thing. It's a piece of cake. We'll take care of everything, and we'll watch Tara. You worry way too much." Those were their parting comments to my flurry of last-minute instructions.

The boys were right. I did worry way too much, but that's the way I am. I think of every possible thing that can go wrong and I try to cover all the bases. But why should I worry? The

barn was secure, and the boys, eighteen and nineteen, were responsible young men. Everything would be fine, I told myself.

We pulled out early the next morning, and I took a last look
at our little spread. Everything was quiet, peaceful, and calm.
Things would be fine while we were gone.

The time flew by in Michigan, and we spent a busy week at
my parent's home with Rick leaving every day to work on my
brother's house about an hour away. They had been able to accomplish a lot working together, and all the walls in the new
family room were now up. Curt had loads of fun with his cousins, and Mom and I got caught up on all the family news and
were able to do some fun shopping.

I called home several times throughout the week to check on
the boys, and they reassured me that all was fine. No, nothing
unusual was happening, and yes, Tara was fine they verified. I
was glad we had decided to make the effort to come after all.

It was dusk when we pulled into our driveway exactly one
week later. Everything looked the same as when we had left:
quiet, peaceful, and calm. I had Rick drop me off at the barn,
and I ran down to check the dogs first thing. The barn was clean
and tidy, and Freeman and the girls, all in their proper pens,
were excitedly jumping up and down to see me. It looked as if
the boys had done a great job.

As the weeks passed, something started to trouble me. It
seemed that Tara was putting on some weight. In fact, she was
getting downright fat. She always did have more of a tendency
to put on weight than our other dogs as she is our shortest dog,
so I pushed my misgivings to the back of my mind.

At first I thought the boys had probably just given her all she
wanted to eat while we were gone, so I was not immediately concerned. However, it's not healthy for a dog to be so fat, so I
promptly put her on a diet. I started giving her about three-fourths
of what she had been used to getting, and she was not a bit happy
about it. She was downright miserable. She turned into a first-rate
thief, stealing food from the other dogs' dishes when their heads
were turned. She went into the garage and pulled down the filled

garbage bags I had piled in the corner where I stored them until they were picked up every Thursday by the trash service. She even climbed the woodpile where I had stowed an especially odorous bag. She licked out all the tin cans in the recycling bin, and I was surprised she didn't slice her tongue open on the razor-sharp edges. And curiously, even with the stringent diet I had her on, she was getting fatter each day. I complained to Rick about it one morning and when he came in that evening after putting the dogs away for the night, he had some shocking news for me.

"Sue...I think Tara is pregnant," he said slowly, raising his eyebrows and fixing me with a sobering look.

I felt my heart skip a beat. "No way, Rick!" I cried. "It's just not possible! The boys watched her closely, and they didn't notice anything unusual." I rambled on. "The dogs were all in their right pens when we came home. If Freeman had bred her, he wouldn't have left her side. He would have still been in there when we came home." I knew that for a fact.

From experience, I know that a male will follow a fertile female around, sticking like glue to her, closer than a shadow and never letting her out of his sight. "And besides," I argued, "how could he have gotten into that pen in the first place?"

"Well, that belly on her is not fat," he insisted. "It's puppies. Maybe someone else bred her."

That comment caused a whole different set of fears to race through my already churning mind. "Oh no," I groaned loudly. "That would be a nightmare. We would have mutts," I wailed. It was every breeder's worst nightmare—mutts! Then I thought for a moment. "The boys would have seen someone hanging around though," I persisted. "She just can't be pregnant, she just can't be!"

The weeks passed and Tara kept getting bigger. It didn't take me long to come to the same conclusion as Rick had, that she really was pregnant. I grimly upped her food ration which met with her wagging, wholehearted approval.

Upon giving the barn a closer inspection, Rick made a discovery. He found a piece of wire mesh that was torn loose at the top right under the ceiling. Freeman would not have been able to reach it from the floor, but by jumping onto the top of his doghouse and leaping up about three feet and then climbing over the wooden beam that separates the two pens, it was remotely possible that he could have gotten into the other pen. Very, very remote, and even if he had, why hadn't the boys ever seen him there? I asked them repeatedly if they had ever spotted him—or anyone else—in that pen. The answer was always no, no, no. No one was ever in that pen except Tara and Meg, they insisted. I know that a male dog simply does not leap three feet up and over to breed and then jump back into his own pen. He would stay with his lady love.

There were no easy answers. We couldn't understand how this had happened, but by this time we would just be thankful if the sire was indeed Freeman and not a roving stray. For if it was possible, remote as it was, that Freeman could have gotten into Tara's pen, it would also have been just as possible for another dog to have done the same thing. It was bad enough that I would have winter Lab pups to take care of; it would be ten times worse if I had mutts of questionable parentage that would be worth almost nothing monetarily. I would have nothing to show for all my hard work.

The weeks passed and Tara was getting larger and larger. The mystery litter would soon be born and we would see who the silent, guilty partner was. Tara's dark velvet eyes could tell me nothing.

One cloudy evening in November, Tara's labor began in earnest. She was stretched out in the whelping box in the basement birthing room, panting hard. I sat down beside her, knowing it was going to be a tiring night for both of us.

As the night wore on, hard contractions started rippling her distended belly, and eventually she started to push.

Would they be purebreds or mongrels? That was the question constantly running through my mind. If the pups were pure Labs, they would be solid colored. In this case with a black mother and a yellow father, (hopefully) there would most likely be some black pups and some yellow pups. If they were spotted, our neighbor's arrogant German Shepherd might be the culprit.

It wasn't long before a thick water sac slid out. As I do at all births, I quickly broke it open to check the pups sucking reflex. If it sucked on my finger, it was alive and healthy. Thankfully, it did, and I gently eased the pup out of the bag. It was a big, totally black male and he was gorgeous. The next one was a smaller yellow female, and there followed five more healthy, squirming, mewing yellow and black purebred pups.

Halfway through the births, I ran upstairs and woke my sleeping husband. "Rick," I whispered loudly. "They're all Labs!" And at that instant, nothing else mattered.

I think every litter of pups we have is extraordinarily beautiful, but for some reason, this litter seemed extra special. For one thing, there was a pale, pale yellow female who was almost white that was simply stunning. We had never had one so light before, and she proved to have one of the sweetest, calmest dispositions we've ever seen. We decided to keep her, and we named her Tara's Rosaleen, Rosie for short. She is now an important part of our future breeding program. Everyone that sees her exclaims about her beauty and presence. The other pups were all healthy and stayed healthy too. They sold surprisingly fast, and I found my dreaded winter-pups vision had not been real at all. Instead, it had come with the unexpected blessing of our sweet Rosie.

To this day, however, every time I'm with Freeman, I picture him in my mind's eye, the perfect gentleman, vaulting back and forth through that torn bit of fencing to visit a welcoming, tail-wagging Tara, doing his husbandly duty and taking care of business, and then leaping back into his own pen with no one the wiser.

Who says you can't teach an old dog new tricks? Ha! They've never met my Freeman!

Chapter 18

I have noticed from time to time that some dog owners, especially new dog owners, have a tendency to humanize their pets. In other words, they tend to think of their dog as a person, with a persons likes and dislikes, emotions, etc., when it really and truly is a dog. Don't get me wrong. Dogs can have wonderful human-like characteristics like being affectionate, loyal, and sensitive, but they are still animals and ultimately behave as such.

A few years ago, we sold a pup to the minister of a local church, Pastor Willis. He was a soft-spoken, likable, middle-aged man who had a pleasant way about him. He was very excited when he picked up his little guy whom he quickly named Lucky. He had a list of questions that he fired off at me and checked off with a red pencil as I answered. I got the impression that he was a perfectionist and wanted to be sure he did everything just right and by the book.

I assured him that I was confident he would do a fine job and as he lived nearby, I encouraged him to stay in touch with us.

A month later, about a week before Valentine's Day, Pastor Willis called. He and Lucky were doing great, he declared, and would like to come over on Valentines Day with a special surprise for Lucky's family. Lucky would come too, as he sorely missed his family, the pastor admitted.

How sweet, I thought to myself, *to think of us and want to bring us a gift.* As an acknowledged chocoholic, visions of creamy chocolate confections danced in my head, and I imagined a varied assortment of possible sweets. After all, what could be more appropriate than candy on Valentine's Day? *Some people are just so thoughtful,* I mused.

Early on Valentine's Day morning, Pastor Willis phoned to ask if early afternoon would be convenient for the family visit.

"Yes, that should work," I assured him as I secretly told my taste buds to prepare themselves for a scrumptious treat.

"Also," Pastor Willis added, "Lucky would like to spend some time with Mama Meg and Papa Freeman, and of course, sister Rose."

Rosie was a sister to Lucky that we had ended up keeping with plans of adding her to our breeding program in the future. He went on. "He misses them so much and just can't wait to see them again!"

I was trying hard not to laugh and to keep my voice as somber as possible. "Why, that would be fine, Pastor Willis," I said in my most serious voice. "However, I do want to warn you not to be disappointed if Freeman and Meg don't recognize Lucky. It's not uncommon for dogs to treat each other just as, well, just as dogs. The reality of them being blood relatives doesn't mean a whole lot to them when they have been separated for a while."

"Oh," Pastor Willis hesitated a moment. I could tell that this new information was a bit unsettling to him. He hadn't allowed for this. He had dreamed and counted on having a happy family reunion, with much tail wagging and nuzzling.

"But it's only been a month since Lucky left your place," he protested. "Surely his parents can't have forgotten him already. I would think they would still remember their little boy."

"Well," I said doubtfully, "I'm almost positive Freeman won't remember him as he wasn't with him all that much and I wouldn't be at all surprised if Meg didn't either. They are animals, you know," I reminded him.

"Just the same," the pastor persisted, "Lucky will stop by later for his visit. And," he declared proudly, "we'll bring our special treat!" He sounded happy and optimistic, and I could tell he really didn't believe me.

The pastor's light blue station wagon rolled onto the driveway at two o'clock. The car door opened and out jumped an older and larger Lucky. He had grown quite a bit in a month and was doing some serious sniffing around the yard, taking in all the enticing smells that only a yard with seven dogs in residence could possibly have. Pastor Willis was all smiles as he walked over and we shook hands. Then he proudly handed me a mysterious brown paper bag.

"Here's the surprise I promised you," he said still beaming broadly. "Happy Valentine's Day!"

It was indeed a real surprise.

"How nice of you to think of us," I gushed. I boldly sniffed the bag, sure I would detect the unmistakable aroma of chocolate, the ultimate valentine in my book.

That's funny, I thought, *the bag doesn't really smell like anything at all.*

I glanced at Pastor Willis who was watching me intently and still beaming. I opened the paper bag carefully, and inside were three small, beautifully wrapped shiny, pink packages with gift cards attached. I curiously opened the first card, and on its shiny cover I read, "Valentine Wishes," surrounded by tiny red and pink hearts. Inside, it read: "To Mama Meg. Wishing you a happy heart always and a wonderful Valentine's Day. Love from your son, Lucky."

I tried hard to wipe off the foolish grin that was trying desperately hard to spread across my face as I opened the fancy little package. Instead of delectable sweets for me, there was a plastic bag filled with five dog bone treats for Mama Meg. The other two cards read the same except one was addressed to Papa Freeman with the same bones as Meg's and the other to Sister Rose which contained miniature dog bones.

I was trying hard to act as if my dogs receiving festively wrapped presents on the holidays were a normal occurrence. The last thing I wanted to do was to make this very nice man feel awkward. *So what if there's no candy,* I consoled myself. It was still a very nice and thoughtful gesture on his part, one that he was not obligated to do.

"What a sweet thing for you to do," I said, giving Pastor Willis my most gallant smile while swallowing my disappointment.

"Just a little something for the family, you know," he chuck-led happily. "Before we leave," he reminded me, "Lucky wants to see his mama, papa, and of course, sister Rose."

"Okay," I replied, shaking my head, "just don't be disap-pointed if they don't recognize each other," I warned him. I walked down to the barn and unlatched the door of the dog pen. Freeman, Meg, and Rosie raced out into the yard and then the circus began. Freeman charged over to Lucky and gave him a long, serious sniff. His upper lip curled back, showing his teeth as he growled menacingly. In his mind, this little guy was a pos-sible competitor and was not to be treated too graciously. Lucky promptly wilted. His ears flattened and his stomach hugged the ground as he waited for the worst. I called to Freeman and led him back to the barn. That was all I needed, Freeman taking a bite out of his son. Then Meg ran up and after sniffing him closely and intently, bristled her thick fur and started to chase Lucky across the yard and up the hill, eyes glaring savagely, a low guttural growl coming from her throat. I could see the pup was scared to death, running for all he was worth, panting heav-ily with his head down and his tail between his legs. I could also see that Meg had no intention of stopping and might get it in her head to chase him across the road to who knows where, so I quickly called her off and walked her back to the barn. Then Rosie decided to add her two cents to the game and jumped up on Lucky, knocking him over. She then started pawing him roughly. Poor Lucky, this was not a lucky day for him.

I looked at Pastor Willis. He stood motionless on the lawn...frozen in shock. I think I could pretty much imagine what he was thinking. How could parents treat their little son in this abominable fashion? What savages! And how could a sister beat up on her brother, showing him no mercy? This was all just too much for his gentle soul to take. I walked over to where the two dogs were still wrestling and pulled Rosie off.

"She just likes to play a little," I said apologetically. "She's really not hurting him," I assured him, hoping I sounded convincing.

I could tell, however, that the good pastor was not convinced. He didn't say a whole lot, but his pleasant face was no longer smiling. Instead, it had a grim, frozen look on it. He quickly gathered up a very tired and most grateful Lucky into his arms and after saying some hasty goodbyes, the two of them left. Our dogs enjoyed the treats, inhaling them in about five seconds flat, barely tasting them. And I guess that Lucky had a change of heart and decided that he really didn't miss his family quite as much as he thought because we never heard from Pastor Willis again.

So much for the Valentine's Day present, I mused. Sometimes things just don't turn out the way we imagine.

Sometimes we simply expect too much from our animal friends. It's good to remind ourselves from time to time that as much as we love them and as wonderful as they are to us, they are still animals...and that's OK.

Chapter 19

Sometimes prospective dog owners have preconceived notions about the best way to care for their new puppy. Some of their information might have come from a friend or an acquaintance, but I have found it usually comes from their own personal ideas of what they themselves think will or will not work. Sometimes the best and most well-meaning intentions of the new owner are not necessarily the best for the dog. This was, in fact, the case when I met a couple named Lisa and Alex.

Lisa called me one afternoon in late summer and, like so many others over the years, said she had seen my ad for puppies and wondered if I happened to have a male pup available. I did, and she enthusiastically assured me that even though she and her husband lived about two hours away, they would try to make it out to our place by dark to have a look at the little guy. I assured her that that would be fine; I would be here.

I have learned throughout the years that the customers' time is my time; whatever works for them has to work for me if I intend to sell anything. Strike while the iron is hot is my motto, while the interest is strong.

Time passed and shadows were beginning to form outside. Since our house is almost impossible to see from the road because of our 600-foot driveway and the small woods separating us from the main road, I turned on the house and barnyard lights, hoping the lights would filter through a little. I knew that driving around in the dark in a strange place looking for an address is not a good feeling.

However, I needn't have worried, for about fifteen minutes later, I could see bright headlights slowly threading their way down the driveway. I breathed a sigh of relief; they had made it!

Lisa and Alex were a friendly young couple in their mid-twenties with two very small children. Marissa, the chubby baby, was four months old and Jesse, the very active older brother, was not quite two.

The children's young ages immediately raised a red flag in my mind. I always hesitate to sell puppies to families with babies or very young children for two reasons. First, there is the simple fact that having a new puppy in the home is very similar to having a new baby in the home. Puppies need almost constant attention and care in the beginning and a lot of time and patience are required. When you have a baby and a puppy, it's like having twins in my book.

Second, is the fact that puppies love to jump on small children. Perhaps it is because they are drawn to a figure their own size and they simply want to play, or maybe it's because they see a small child as just another toy to chew on. Regardless of the reason, they see nothing wrong with tugging and chewing on the unsuspecting youngster's clothing and nipping at their hands and feet with their needle-sharp baby teeth.

This is just normal puppy behavior, but it can intimidate and scare young children, which is not what you want. I would rather discourage prospective buyers and lose a sale up front than deal with an unhappy and frustrated owner a month later. So I decided to let them know my feelings immediately.

Alex was busy playing with the attention-loving pups while Lisa was trying in vain to quiet the baby who was starting to fuss. Jesse had grown tired of the puppies after the first few minutes and was now making himself at home in our toy corner, surrounding himself with an array of Legos and a fleet of miniature cars and trucks that belonged to our youngest son.

Looking at Alex and Lisa intently, I said in my most serious voice, "You know, I usually try to discourage families as young as yours from getting a puppy."

Alex's brow wrinkled and his eyes questioned me as he tried to fathom why I didn't want to sell them a puppy. I continued, "I know you haven't had a dog before, and believe me, I'm not discriminating against you, but take it from me, they're a lot of work. It would be," and here I looked at Lisa meaningfully, "it would be," I repeated, "like having another child." I waited a moment, giving time for my words to sink in and then went on.

"Another thing, puppies like to play rough. They like to jump, and they can and will bite if they have the chance. That can be scary, especially for smaller kids,"

I warned. "Maybe it wouldn't hurt to wait until your kids get a little older before you take this step," I suggested.

"Oh, you don't have to worry about us," Lisa declared vehemently with a surprised look on her pretty face.

"We've given this a lot of thought, haven't we Alex?" She turned and looked across at her husband beseechingly.

"Sure have," Alex agreed complacently. "We realize it'll take some time and work, but we're ready. We really believe it's a good idea to have a dog grow up with the kiddies," he said as he glanced over at Jesse, happily rolling a truck across the carpet. "That way they'll be real friends."

Since their minds were obviously made up, I gave in. "I'm not saying it can't work," I said, defending myself. "I'm just warning you. I want you to know what you're getting into. After all, I want you to be happy. I've had several experiences in the past where new owners called me at their wits end when the pup turned out to be more of an undertaking than they had bargained for."

"Don't worry about us, we'll be fine," they assured me once more as they smiled at me rather indulgently. "We've waited a long time for this day," Alex added. They quickly decided which pup they wanted, and we sat down at the dining room table to go over the necessary paperwork.

This was the time I always gave new owners my "new puppy lecture," advice and common sense on care and training for the new addition to the family. After living with dogs almost my entire life and breeding and raising them for many years, I believed that there really was nothing like experience.

"One very important item I wholeheartedly recommend to all puppy owners is a crate to keep the pup in at night, and when you're not at home during the day," I said seriously, meeting Alex's suddenly shocked gaze.

"You mean we have to keep the puppy in a cage?" Alex asked, disbelief echoing in his voice. "We can't do that! It's going to be a member of the family," he said pointedly, catching his wife's eye.

"That seems so cruel," nodded his wife, rocking noisy Marissa back and forth as she went and stood behind him.

"It's really not as bad as it sounds," I said calmly. "We call it a crate, not a cage," I corrected, "and eventually most dogs come to love it." I explained further, "The crate becomes the dog's own private room, you might say, its own space. He'll feel secure in there. When he needs to get away from the kids or you or wants to take a nap, he'll have a place to go to. He'll use it as a sort of retreat.

"One more thing," I added, "when the pup is in his crate, he'll try his very hardest to keep it clean for the simple reason that it's his. And remember, while the pup is in its crate, your furniture and chair legs, as well as your shoes, are safe from sharp little teeth," I concluded in my most convincing voice.

The room was totally quiet except for baby Marissa's fussing. No one said a word. Finally Alex glanced at me furtively, and I knew he was not happy.

"We just can't do it," Alex said with fierce resolve in his young voice. "It just doesn't seem right," he said earnestly.

"Yes, I agree, it seems so cruel," Lisa repeated, nodding her head. "We have a nice big mud room where the washer and dryer are that the puppy can sleep in at night. He'll have plenty of room in there and I'll keep a close eye on him during the day," she added conscientiously.

I sighed. It was so hard to change firmly made up minds, but I had tried. "I don't recommend it, but you can try it that way if you want and see how it works," I counseled. "It may work just fine, you never know."

I really hoped it did for their sakes, but I had my doubts. I hadn't been raising dogs for years for nothing. I knew puppies.

We talked a bit more and after retrieving Jesse from the toys, Alex scooped up the pup in his long arms and walked to the door. Lisa waved goodbye, and I wished them good luck. "Remember," I called as they were getting into their car, "if you have a question about something, don't hesitate to call me. I only take my phone off the hook the first night a puppy leaves," I joked. "And after the first night, you should be all set," I added encouragingly.

Three days later the phone rang in mid-afternoon. When I answered it I thought I recognized Lisa's voice, but it sounded different, strained and a bit desperate.

"Sue, we're having some real problems," she admitted wearily. "We just don't know what to do. We don't know if we can keep him."

"Tell me what's happening," I said, wondering what on earth had happened.

"Well, the pup is a real sweetheart," she admitted.

"We named him Duke and he's super all day. It's night time that's the problem. At ten o'clock the first night, we took him outside one last time to go to the bathroom, you know, like you said. Then I put him in the mud room with a blanket and some of his toys and closed the door. I did leave the light on, too," she allowed. "I didn't want him to be scared of the dark. He began crying and whining and just wouldn't stop. We did like you said though and let him tough it out. We didn't run to him and tried our hardest to ignore him. But he cried for three hours straight," she said in a stunned voice. "Three hours," she repeated. "It was like he was scared or something. He whined and cried and howled from ten o'clock until one in the morning and all four of us were wide awake the whole entire time," she added tiredly.

"And that wasn't even the worst of it. When we checked him this morning, we found that he had messed five different times in five different places. What a mess!" she sighed as she continued her sad tale. "I cleaned the room and gave Duke a bath; you can't imagine what he looked like."

She was wrong there. I could imagine only too well. Lisa continued. "Then we thought that maybe this was a one-time thing, that it happened because everything was new and strange to him. But last night was the same thing, the same crying, and the same mess. We really don't know what to do. I do know that we can't keep going on like this though." Her voice sounded as if it were ready to break.

Part of me felt like saying, *I told you so*, but I was good. I didn't. I was doing some fast thinking. She had said the pup sounded scared. Well, he probably was.

"Lisa, do me a favor," I pleaded. "Go get a crate today. Duke needs to feel secure and the crate will help. Also, leave the light off. Dogs can see in the dark, you know."

"Do you really think it will make any difference?" she asked doubtfully. "It seems too simple."

"Yes, Lisa, I really do," I said firmly. "Give it a try," I urged. "You've got nothing to lose."

I could hear her take a deep breath. "You're right, Sue. At this point, I'm willing to try anything."

She promised to keep in touch and let me know how things went. I earnestly hoped the situation would improve, as much for the dog's sake as for theirs.

This is all they need, I thought, shaking my head incredulously, two small children and a dirty, crying puppy.

The next day, my first thought upon waking was wondering how the night had gone for Lisa and Alex. I didn't have long to wait before the phone rang and sure enough, it was Lisa. "Sue," she said excitedly. "You won't believe what happened last night."

Okay, I thought, *now what?*

"We did like you said and bought a plastic cage, I mean a crate," she corrected herself, "for Duke at the feed store. He cried a little when we first put him in it at night, but he quieted down after about ten minutes. Ten minutes!" she repeated, "and he never made another sound all night," she said incredulously.

"Why that's wonderful, Lisa," I exclaimed, and I couldn't help it, I was grinning from ear to ear. Yes! I was right, I was right, I crowed to myself!

"But that's not all," she went on. "His crate was perfectly clean this morning!" I could hear the exultation in her voice. "We can scarcely believe it," she confessed happily. "We just love him!"

Yes, I allowed, a clean, quiet puppy is a bit easier to love than a dirty, noisy one.

I was genuinely thrilled that things had worked out so well, but I was not really surprised. It was only common sense. The crate and the dark room had helped the pup feel safe and secure as if he were in his own cozy den. And he certainly wouldn't want to make a mess in the crate as he had no way of getting away from it as he had in the mud room. He didn't want to sit in a small, stinky area, so he had forced himself to wait patiently until he could go outside in the morning and do his job.

Who says animals are dumb? They prove over and over again that they are so much smarter than we give them credit for. We just have to remind ourselves to look at things through *their* eyes and try to think as they would.

Yes, I reminded myself with a pat on the back, *there is something to be said for a little experience.*

Chapter 20

My fellow Lab breeder, Eva Sanders had a problem that was the secret horror of every serious dog breeder. Eva had an infertile female. The very fact that Eva would even admit that she had a dog that was less than perfect was something in itself. Eva's pride and joy were her dogs. Her life revolved around them. Their champion pedigrees and perfect looks meant the world to her. And indeed, they were very nice dogs to be sure, but listening to Eva incessantly sing their praises got to be a bit much after awhile.

Crystal, Eva's female, was an unusually appealing creature. She came from very respectable bloodlines; her parents had been imported from England. She looked and acted like a princess with classic good looks and a noble bearing. Her coat was pale yellow with darker yellow shades highlighting her soft fur. And perhaps most important of all, she had a sweet, eager-to-please disposition that caused all who met her to love her.

One day when Crystal was around two or so, I happened to see Eva and asked her if she planned on breeding Crystal in the near future. Two seems to be the magic age when most breeders usually start their dogs, as it takes until then for them to fully mature.

Her response was typical of what I had come to expect from Eva. She tossed her jet black head at me and fixed me with her penetrating, all-knowing eyes. "Well, it may surprise you, Sue, but I have already been looking for a mate for Crystal," she admitted a bit arrogantly. "But," she continued, looking at me severely, "he has to be someone quite special you know. The right pedigree, of course, and champions in the background are a must." She paused as she thought for a moment and then went on. "I do have my eye on a couple of studs though. They're both up north. One is in Vermont, and the other is in New Hampshire."

Of course, there's nobody local that's good enough for you, I thought to myself.

She sighed languidly as she continued, "I've been talking to their owners, and they seem to be serious possibilities. Of course, I haven't actually seen them yet, but if they're as nice as they sound, we may be interested. I can't breed Crystal to just anyone, you know."

Yes, I suppose I did know that. I owned two very nice yellow studs—at least I thought they were nice. They weren't show quality dogs, but not many dogs are. However, they were good, healthy guys who consistently produced great family pets, which are what ninety-nine percent of customers want.

I knew that in Eva's mind, my males not only didn't rate as possibilities, they were not even to be considered. I wished Eva good luck and thought to myself, *This will be one litter of pups I will have to make sure I see. With Lady Crystal for the mother and a champion show dog for the sire, it just can't get any better. What could possibly go wrong with that plan?*

A year went by before I chanced to meet Eva again and after some small talk, I asked about Crystal. "Has she had any pups yet?"

Eva's chiseled, patrician features bore a troubled look as she gazed down at me. "Funny that you should ask," she said. "We did try breeding Crystal to this male in Vermont who was totally gorgeous, and I mean totally gorgeous." She rolled her eyes as she thought back. "He was a multiple show champion and all, you know," she gushed. "But for some reason, Crystal wouldn't let him breed her. She kept sitting down. She just didn't like him," she said with bewilderment showing in her cultured voice. "So we ended up doing AI on her."

AI stands for artificial insemination, which is getting to be more and more common in the dog-breeding business. Semen is collected from the male and inserted into the vaginal tract of the female, via a syringe, midway through her heat cycle when she is most fertile. When done properly, this procedure has the same results as a natural breeding.

Eva continued, "That didn't work either," she said with a sigh. "I just don't know what the problem is. The stud has sired other litters so the problem doesn't seem to be his," she granted. "I'm just going to have to try again with her next heat. Sometimes these things take time, you know," she concluded.

I nodded. I did know. I had gone through some stressful times a few years before with one of our own dogs, Trixie, who we thought was sterile until she surprised us with a beautiful litter of ten pups.

Months passed and I didn't see Eva again for almost two years, but she was the same as ever when we met. We visited a bit, and then I broached the question I had wondered about from time to time, "Did Crystal ever have any pups?" I asked curiously.

Eva's face darkened for a moment as she stared intently at me. "No, as a matter of fact, she hasn't, and we can't understand why," she said dejectedly. "You remember how we bred her using AI to that stud up in Vermont?"

I nodded; I remembered.

"Well, we took her up there during her next heat and tried again with the same results. So then we decided to try a stud in New Hampshire. He was a beauty. and his bloodlines were..." and her eyes lit up for a moment.

"But the same thing happened," she said with a frown.

"No way," I said unbelievingly. "Again?"

She drew a hand across her brow wearily. "Yes, the same thing. Crystal wouldn't let him breed her. She acted exactly like she did with that other stud from Vermont."

She sighed again. "So, we ended up doing AI on her again, with no results," she added sadly. "I hate to think of it, but there must be something wrong with her. When I think of all the time and effort I've spent carting her back and forth to Vermont and New Hampshire...." Her voice trailed off. "She's not getting any younger either, you know."

I did know that older moms were sometimes apt to have more birthing problems than younger tip-top shape ones.

But I had an idea, an idea I had been thinking about for some time and I decided it was now or never. So I mustered up all my courage and went ahead. "Eva," I began hesitantly, "I know you really want some puppies out of Crystal, and well..." I paused, but made myself go on. "We have two studs at our place, remember? I realize they don't have the pedigrees that those males up north have, but we do only live fifteen miles away. It would be a whole lot easier."

I could see Eva staring at me with her eyes opened wide and her prim mouth partly open as if she could scarcely believe what she was hearing. The nerve I had! Oh, well, the damage was already done so I blundered on. "You could drop her off at my place when she comes in heat again and leave her as long as you like. Who knows?" I added encouragingly, "It just might work!"

Eva was still staring at me, and I could tell by the slightly shocked expression on her face exactly what she was thinking.

I know, who am I to think my ordinary, very average guys are good enough for Miss Crystal?

"Uh...well, I'll have to think about it, Sue," she managed to say as she looked off in the distance somewhere, unable, or perhaps unwilling, to meet my eyes. "I may just try her with another male I've had my eye on."

Our conversation soon dwindled, and we said our goodbyes.

Well, that's that, I thought. I hadn't accomplished anything, but I had tried.

So I was more than a little surprised when about a year later, Eva called and wondered if she could bring Crystal over. She was in season again, and Eva was willing to try one of our males with her. I knew it had taken a lot for Eva to make that call and that some amount of pride had to have been swallowed, but I was elated! I felt I had finally passed some imaginary, yet very real test. However, I also fully realized that I was the absolute last resort.

The next day, Eva drove over in her latest new car with Crystal enthroned in the backseat, peering curiously out of the window. After inspecting both studs, Eva decided on Lion, my own personal favorite. I assured Eva that I would keep a close eye on Crystal and would keep in touch with her to let her know of any developments.

"Think positive," I encouraged her as she walked to her car. "You never know!"

She looked at me doubtfully, and it wasn't hard to see that she had some serious misgivings about this whole set-up.

Love at first sight seems like a line from a fairy tale, but that's exactly what it was. Lion was at his best as he wooed and nuzzled Crystal. And Crystal—well, she followed him around like a shadow, pressing against him lovingly. I could tell we were going to have a genuine honeymoon on our hands here in no time flat.

And I was right. It wasn't long before there was a tie. Lion was the first dog she had ever allowed to mate her. I almost jumped up and down in my excitement as I ran to the phone to call Eva and give her the good news. I was surprised and a bit disappointed that she wasn't as ecstatic as I was. In fact, she was pessimistic about the whole thing. "Just because he bred her doesn't mean she's going to get pregnant," she warned me darkly.

I knew that of course, but I was feeling optimistic. I just had a hunch. They stayed together for about a week longer before the honeymoon came to an abrupt end. It was time for Eva to pick up her girl. I gave Crystal a final pat on the head and told Eva to be sure and keep me posted. She would, she said, but it was plain to see she still had her doubts.

From conception to birth takes between sixty and sixty-five days. That's about nine weeks. Labs and other large-boned breeds tend to carry their pups under their rib cage at first, so it is almost impossible to tell if a female is pregnant until she's between five and six weeks along because then the pups start spreading out as they become larger. It had been over a month since Crystal left our place, and I continued to be optimistic, but I had to know for sure.

I called Eva and my bubble burst. She had some disappointing news. "She's not a bit bigger," she declared. "I didn't think she would take anyway," she said gloomily.

"You never know," I pressed, "her abdominal muscles are tight from never having had pups before. It might take a little longer for her to really show."

The phone rang exactly four days later, and a new, excited Eva was on the other end. "She's definitely got something in there, Sue," she exclaimed loudly in my ear. "All at once, she just seemed to pop! She's definitely pregnant!"

I knew it! It seemed my gut feeling had been right all along. Lion was going to be a father once again.

Three weeks later, the phone rang early in the morning. This was the call I had been waiting for. A tired sounding, but proud Eva announced, "Crystal's been in labor all night and you'll never believe it! She has nine gorgeous puppies! They all look exactly like her, five females and four males." She went on and on. I immediately picked up on the fact that the pups looked exactly like their lovely mother without a word mentioned about their handsome father, my Lion, but that was okay. I was willing to give her that much. "They are just too precious," she cooed.

I was thrilled; thrilled for Eva who had wanted these puppies so badly and for so long, thrilled for Crystal who would make a wonderful mother, and thrilled for myself. After all, *my* dog was the sire of these marvelous, miracle pups.

My very nice, but very average, Lion had been able to accomplish what studs of renown had not. And Eva was so pleased with the way the pups turned out that she ended up breeding Crystal two more times to Lion, each breeding producing litters of fine healthy pups.

Yes, fancy pedigrees and fancy looks are great, I thought to myself as I reflected back on the whole Crystal-Lion affair, *but sometimes it takes just an average, everyday guy to get the job done right.*

Chapter 21

I had a serious problem on my hands. For some unexplained reason, one of Licorice's newborn puppies refused to nurse. And it didn't take too many brains to figure out that something would have to be done soon if the pup was to survive.

I had spent most of the day sitting next to Licorice as she delivered eight beautiful pups. All of our pups are beautiful, I like to think, but Licorice was our very first dog. She was the one who got us started in this special business and so she seemed to be extra special to me and, by extension, her pups too. She was black and we had bred her to our yellow stud, Lion, so it was no surprise to see the outcome: five yellow and three black pups. Perched on the edge of the wooden whelping box in the basement, I decided that they were a perfect looking, even-sized bunch of pups. No runts in this litter. I stroked Licorice's soft head and whispered gently, "You did it again, Licorice. You've got some nice babies there."

She looked up at me with weary eyes, tired from her hours of labor and travail, but serene in the knowledge that she was the responsible mother and sole provider to eight new beings that depended on her totally.

Our Lab moms have tremendous maternal instincts. They are never as satisfied and content as when they have a litter of pups tucked in close to their bellies, blissfully nursing away. In fact, once when I was concerned that Tara had not fully regained her strength from a previous litter, I decided not to breed her when her next heat rolled around. Instead, we skipped it and planned on breeding her when she came in season again.

All was well and good until her sister Trixie had a litter of pups six weeks later. Tara decided that if she couldn't have pups of her own, she would just take Trixie's, plain and simple. Whenever I opened the door to the puppy room to let Trixie out for a breath of fresh air and a little exercise, Tara would be waiting as close to that door as she could possibly get. I had to hold onto her with an iron grip to keep her from charging inside. Once, when I let my guard down for just a second, she bolted into the room before I could get the door closed, and stood guard over her sister's puppies, sniffing each pup in turn and even giving them an occasional lick. Ten minutes later, when Trixie wanted back in the room with her babies, Tara wouldn't budge. Her fur bristled, and a low growl came from deep in her throat. She wanted those pups and she wasn't giving them up easily. I had to forcefully remove her from the room so a worried Trixie could reclaim her progeny.

We have found that if we skip a female's heat, she will sometimes come into her next heat in four months instead of the usual six months. It seems they just crave those puppies and will do whatever it takes to get them.

Whenever new puppies are born, I always make sure each one nurses as soon after birth as possible in order to receive the precious colostrum, the first milk that contains the all-important maternal antibodies that protect the pups against infection and disease. Usually this is not a problem as newborn pups are born with a wonderful sucking instinct and immediately after birth, they wriggle around pressing their sightless heads this way and that, rooting around for a milk-engorged nipple even before they are dried off.

Under my careful scrutiny, seven pups had nursed well. In fact, they were pulling on those nipples as though they were starving. They gave little contented gasps and groans as they sucked the precious, life-giving fluid. Yes, seven were fine but it was the eighth pup that I was worried about, a pug-nosed yellow female. I watched her closely. Her mouth would close on a nipple and then slide off as though she was immensely tired. This was not normal behavior. I put my index finger into her mouth, and where a normal puppy will suck on it for all he's worth, this pup just sort of played with my finger with her tongue.

I had an inkling right then that something wasn't quite right. But I had never run into this problem before, so I decided she probably just needed a little help, a little enticement. I found her a nice fat milky nipple and placed her mouth around it. No response. Her mouth slid off and there was no connection made. She made pathetic little whimpering sounds and I knew that she was growing not only frustrated, but hungry too. I also knew that without nourishment soon, the pup would go downhill fast, and I wasn't used to losing puppies. I couldn't deal with loss. My pups always lived and were healthy. If they didn't start out so healthy, I worked on them until they became healthy.

I decided to try feeding the pup with a tiny bottle, made especially for newborn kittens and puppies that needed to be bottle fed. I mixed up some puppy formula that I had gotten from the local feed store and filled the bottle. I poked the tiny nipple into the pup's mouth. Nothing. No normal sucking reflex at all.

Well, I thought optimistically, whatever problem this little girl has, perhaps she will outgrow it in time. Maybe her system is just a little immature. I was positive I could cure her of whatever ailed her, so I decided to tube feed her and see what happened. Tube feeding is the method of choice when you are dealing with a sick puppy that is too weak to nurse naturally or an immature puppy whose sucking reflex hasn't developed fully. It's a very easy procedure—once you've done it a few times, that is—and takes about two minutes to complete. You insert a soft rubber tube into the puppy's mouth and pass the tube over its tongue and down the throat to the pup's stomach where you will feel a bit of resistance. At this point, you slowly inject a syringe filled with formula into the tube, which will drain into the puppy's stomach. I held the squirming pup firmly in my hands and proceeded to tube feed. It went well, and the pup seemed quieter and more contented.

Every day I would first try to get the pup to nurse on Licorice, but the results were disheartening and I would eventually resort to tube feeding. I still could not detect any sucking reflex, but I blindly continued to believe that the pup would outgrow her problem in time and that everything would be fine. That's what kept me going during those dreary, middle-of-the-night feedings when I was weary and half asleep.

Other breeders lose puppies, but I don't, I reminded myself. I went the extra mile and took special care of my babies and watched them like a hawk. I couldn't lose this puppy; I was trying too hard. I was doing all I could, and didn't that count for something? I fed the pup every three to four hours day and night, and there was no denying that the little girl was growing. Yes, slightly growing but not thriving. There is a difference.

I didn't want to face the very real fact that the pup was getting progressively weaker. Six days had gone by, and she was only half the size of her siblings. I was very worried and finally came to the realization that something was very wrong.

On the morning of the seventh day, I called Anne, a good friend of mine who is also a fellow breeder and has been in the business far longer than I. I cried on her shoulder for a few minutes and told her the whole sad story.

Anne listened and then asked me a curious question. "Sue, have you ever looked at the inside of the pup's mouth?"

"Why no, I haven't," I said, taken back a bit. "What should I look for?" I asked.

Aren't all mouths the same? I wondered.

"Make sure the roof of her mouth is okay. I was just thinking she might have a cleft palate," Anne said in a low tone. "And if it's that, it could be serious." Her voice sounded ominous.

I didn't even know what a cleft palate was, but it sounded bad. I hurriedly pulled my well worn Vet Handbook out from the bookcase and thumbed to the chapter on cleft palates. I read the article, hardly believing what I was reading. The article told me some things I didn't want to know.

"Cleft palate is a birth defect that is caused by the failure of the bones of the upper mouth to form completely. Many times it is impossible for the puppy to create enough suction to nurse."

I slammed the book shut and raced down to the basement room where Licorice and her pups were laying spread out in the whelping box. I picked up the small pup once more and opened her mouth gingerly. I was shocked! I could scarcely believe what I saw. Instead of the roof of her mouth being smooth and in one complete piece, it was divided into two sections. It had a fissure, a large crack going through the middle of it, an opening that was about a quarter-inch wide.

This is a cleft palate, I told myself. *I'm looking at it right now.*

No wonder she hadn't been able to nurse with that slit in her mouth. I could see that corrective surgery was not even an option in this case because of the severity of the deformity. I stood there in shock, not wanting to accept what I had just seen. I slowly placed the tiny pup back in the box next to her healthy, vigorous siblings and thought long and hard. I had to resign myself to the fact that this helpless pup would soon die, and that all of my heroic efforts had been in vain.

Sometimes we believe we can change fate and make things turn out right, that a difficult situation can be reversed. We make ourselves believe that if we try hard enough and do our best, we can fix anything. Sometimes we can. In reality though, there are times when a fix is not available or even possible. Sometimes life dishes out some pretty unpleasant situations when even our best is not good enough. Some things are simply out of our control, and it is best, I've found, if we can just somehow accept it and let go.

After all, this is life, I continually remind myself, *where disappointments can and do happen*. In the animal world, the strong survive, and the weak die, and it happens for a reason. I've come to the conclusion that I must accept the things that I don't understand and go on...for life does go on.

Chapter 22

"You do have two females left?" That was the anxious question being asked by the deep-voiced caller on the phone one Wednesday afternoon in late November.

"Yes, I do," I answered. I had sold three pups out of Meg's latest litter, and I had four left. They were eight weeks old and ready to go. Hopefully, this guy would make it only three.

"I think we're very interested," the deep voice went on. "My name's Mike Kendall. We have a fourteen-year-old dog. She's a mix, part German Shepherd and part wolf." His voice suddenly changed; it sounded strained for some reason. He continued. "Her name's Emma, and we're...we're going to have her put to sleep on Saturday."

"Oh, that's too bad," I murmured sympathetically.

"What happened?"

"Well, she's been having trouble walking," Mike continued in a subdued voice. "Her back legs keep going out on her; she's got arthritis in them pretty bad, so it's time. The vet said there's nothing he can do for her." There was silence for a moment. Then he continued. "It's going to be awful tough though," he admitted. "She grew up with the kids; we've got two girls, four and twelve," he explained. "She never once was mean or nippy to them." His voice sounded thick, as though he had a bad cold, but I knew better. "She's been a wonderful dog." He stopped and I could hear him clearing his throat. His voice trembled slightly as he continued.

"We have these neighbors next door and the husband loves Emma as much as we do. She spends about as much time at his house as she does at ours. He's going to miss her too," he said, as his voice softened, heavy with emotion. Then he seemed to make a conscious effort to pull himself back together, and he remembered why he had called.

"Like I was saying, I am interested in a female. My wife, Kathy, and I think it would be best if we got another dog right away. We're so used to a dog being around all the time," he explained. "And then we've been thinking it might be easier on the girls if we get a puppy right away that they can train and play with, something to take their minds off of Emma," he explained.

"I think that's a good idea," I said encouragingly.

And I really did. When the heart is full and breaking, there is nothing like a happy-go-lucky, tail-wagging puppy to make you stop feeling sorry for yourself. I also think it's sometimes a wise idea to get a dog that is totally different from the previous one, either a different breed of dog or even just a different color. That way, you won't be so tempted to compare the two.

"Could we stop by, in say an hour from now?" Mike asked. "We'll bring our younger daughter with us. The older one is in school and won't be home for a while yet."

I looked at the kitchen clock. "That works for me," I allowed. "I'll see you then," and I hung the receiver up.

This is what a dog does to you, I reminded myself. *They make you fall in love with them and then break your heart when they leave. And when they do go, a part of you seems to go right along with them, and there's an ache and a void there that only another dog can fill.*

I've seen it happen time after time. It's funny how we're made, I speculated, made with so many intense emotions and such a capacity to feel and to love. Granted, animals are not human, but at times we can feel closer to them than to another person.

Exactly one hour later, there was a heavy knock on the backdoor and a pleasant looking, sad-eyed man in his thirties firmly shook my hand and introduced himself as Mike. Close behind him was his wife, Kathy, a slim, vivacious looking woman, and Kari, their cute, blonde four year old. When I opened the door, Lion and Meg, who were keeping me company in the house, immediately slipped out to greet them. The Kendalls enthusiastically began petting them and it was easy to see they were genuine animal lovers.

As we started to walk down to the barn, Kathy began apologizing for her red, swollen eyes. "I've been crying for an hour straight. It seems all I do anymore is cry," she confessed. "Just thinking about putting Emma down..."

Her voice broke, and we walked faster in the icy, stinging air. "I go back and forth," she said dolefully, "should we or shouldn't we? She'll go for a couple of days and be pretty good, and I'll think she's okay, that she's going to make it, but then all of a sudden, her back legs will just go flat out on her, and she can't get up without one of us helping her. And then lately, she's having trouble controlling her bowels, too. Oh, it's just so pathetic!" She sighed deeply, and I could see the tears creeping into the corners of her swollen eyes again.

We had reached the barn now, and I walked over to the puppy room door and swung it wide. Sudden smiles lit up three dreary faces as they bent over the puppies. I located the two females and placed them on the barn floor where they started running around in circles, thrilled with their newfound freedom. One of the pups was fairly light in color while the other was much darker, almost a reddish-brown color. Kathy watched both pups closely and impulsively scooped up the darker one and declared, "This is the one I want! What do you think, Mike?"

Mike nodded his head in complete agreement. It was plain to see that Mike was a complacent, easygoing guy and that whatever made his wife happy, made him happy too. Kathy held the cuddly pup tight in her arms and brought its pudgy face close to hers. The pup pressed its moist nose against her face and gave it a sloppy lick with its warm pink tongue. Kathy's eyes were shining; this was definitely the one.

Then, still holding the lucky pup, she turned to me with a brave, quivering smile. "You know, we bought Emma right after we were first married, over fourteen years now," she said, glancing at her husband with a pensive look. She paused for a moment to clear her throat and then continued. "We hadn't planned on getting a dog...but it just...it just happened. I can't explain it. We were driving past this little pet store, and we just stopped in, spur of the moment you know. And there she was!" She was silent for a moment, and her eyes had a faraway, distant look in them. I knew she was going back fourteen years in time when she and her husband had been so young and so in love. I knew she was visualizing the small, fluffy puppy that had captivated their hearts.

She laughed suddenly, remembering. "You know, we had all this wedding money in our pockets, and we suddenly decided we wanted her...so we bought her!" she exclaimed. "She was so cute. We brought her home and she was good, good right from the start. And our neighbor, he loved her so much too. If Emma wasn't at our house, she'd be at his. He feels terrible about this whole thing, almost as bad as we do. In fact, he wants to bury Emma halfway between our two houses."

She took a deep breath before she continued. "We've thought and thought, and we know we're doing the right thing. It's just that we're going to miss her so much," she admitted as a lone tear trickled down the side of her cheek. She wiped her wet eyes with her sleeve and gently put the yellow pup down on the floor and walked over to where her silent husband was standing.

"Do you really like the one I picked?" she asked with a tremor in her voice as she looked up at him.

"I sure do," Mike said resolutely. His face looked determined and his voice was unwavering. "It'll be the best thing for us Kathy, and good for the kids too."

This seemed to remind him of something, and he glanced over at me. "Sue, would it be all right if, before we make the final decision, we bring our other daughter over to look at the pups?"

"Oh, yes," Kathy agreed. "We want Jenny, that's our other daughter, to be part of this. This has to be a family decision," she explained.

"That's fine with me," I agreed. My day was open, and I had no pressing plans.

"We'll be back with Jenny in about an hour and a half," Mike said as he checked his watch and leaned over to give the pup a final pat.

I picked the pup up and held her small face close to mine. "You've got some awfully big shoes to fill," I warned her. Then I put her back in the room with her envious siblings who were trying their hardest to climb out of the room.

"Just be sure you don't sell her on us," Kathy warned as she dabbed at her still puffy eyes with a sodden Kleenex as we left the barn.

I assured her I wouldn't and walked back up to the house, watching their car drive slowly down the driveway.

Exactly an hour and a half later the Kendalls returned with their daughter Jenny, a cute, intelligent looking twelve year old. We made the familiar trip to the barn once again and as I placed the two pups on the floor, Jenny immediately pointed at the darker one and announced just as her mother had a few hours earlier, "I want that one."

I breathed a sigh of relief. This was going to be easy. For once everyone wanted the same one. We stood there in the barn for a while, with the four of them taking turns holding and petting the lucky pup, the pup that was being bought to fill the tremendous void another would make.

Then Mike turned to me and said quietly, "We made an appointment at the vet's for Emma on Saturday at one p.m. Do you think we should take the puppy with us now or wait...wait until after...?"

I thought for only a second. "I think if I were you, I would let Emma spend the precious time she has left with just her family," I said slowly. "A noisy puppy pulling on her and distracting you is not what any of you need right now. Just give Emma all of your attention."

Kathy's eyes started to spill over once more, and a muffled sob escaped her. She turned away from me suddenly. "It's so hard," she whispered, her voice thick with emotion.

"I know," I said with all the firmness I could muster, "but it's only going to get worse. You know that."

"Yes, I know. I can tell she's in pain now," she admitted, blowing her nose in a wrinkled hanky she had fished out of her coat pocket.

"Kathy, it's the right thing to do," Mike urged gently.

"We've been over this a hundred times. She's fourteen years old; she's had a good life."

"I know, I know," Kathy repeated as we left the barn. "It just doesn't make it any easier, you know."

"Our appointment at the vet's is at 1:00 p.m.," Mike said again, turning to me. "We'll plan on being back here at 3:00 p.m." They walked silently to their car, probably thinking of all that had to take place between now and then, and drove off.

Yes, it isn't always easy to do what you know should be done, I thought. *Your mind tells you one thing and your heart tells you something else.* It wasn't going to be easy, that was for sure, and I was thankful I wasn't in their shoes.

When I woke up Saturday morning came my first thoughts were of the Kendalls. I said a silent prayer that God would be with them this day as I went about my work. I brought their pup in from the barn and gave her a bath and put her in the big dog crate in the dining room which was reserved for clean, departing pups.

The hours slowly passed, and a little after 3:00 o'clock the Kendalls drove in. I motioned them inside, and Kathy and Mike walked into the kitchen. Kathy's face was a mess, and she was sobbing uncontrollably.

Mike stood in the doorway and in a strange, unnatural voice said slowly, "You know, that's the hardest thing I've ever done in my whole life." He wiped his eyes with the back of his hand and looked over my head at something only he could see.

The silence was long and awkward. The only thing I could think to do was to hand them the pup, so I did. Kathy held it clumsily for a moment, and then I took it back from her. I could see she was having a very hard time.

Mike just stood by the kitchen table, his face twisted with grief. "That's got to be the hardest thing I ever did in my life," he repeated, his eyes searching the floor. "To hold her in my arms and feel the life flowing right out of her." He shook his head. "We buried her right between the two houses, ours and the neighbor's. Our neighbor, he helped me dig the hole, and we buried her there together. He went to the vet's with us too and he even came along with us here," he said as he pointed out the window.

What a neighbor, I thought to myself. I hadn't even known anyone was waiting outside. I could plainly see they both wanted to get going. Talk was painful and words were useless. I quickly went over the puppy registration form with Kathy, but my words were wasted on her. She wasn't listening. Her thoughts were far away and I knew she was once again seeing the lovable puppy they had brought home fourteen years ago that was no more.

I handed the perky pup to Mike and suggested that he take her outside so she could go to the bathroom before they started on their ride home. He nodded and walked out of the kitchen with the puppy clasped tightly in his arms.

I turned to Kathy who was fighting heroically to keep the tears at bay, but it wasn't working. She angrily wiped her eyes, not daring to meet mine. I put my arm around her and said softly, "Kathy, it will only get better; today is the absolute worst it can get."

She stared at me with unseeing eyes and said, "You know, she was coming up the porch stairs to the house this morning, and her back legs collapsed. She just lay there. I had to go help her." She burst into a flood of tears again.

"That happened for a reason," I said firmly.

She looked at me questioningly.

"You had to see how bad she really was once more so you could let her go." She nodded, sniffling. "You have to remember," I said firmly, "that you gave her a wonderful life."

We walked outside, and there was the light-hearted pup racing around on the gravel driveway, completely oblivious to the gloomy atmosphere. Mike quickly introduced me to the quiet, unassuming middle-aged man with the downcast face who was standing next to him. It was the neighbor, the faithful neighbor. He looked at me with deep pain in his dark eyes and simply said one word as his eyes met mine.

"Transition," he said softly. His sorrowful eyes followed the lively pup running at his feet, and then he turned away.

Yes, I thought—transition; it was never easy.

We said our good-byes quickly. There was too much hurt, too much newness. It would take some time. Something lingered in the back of my mind all the rest of the day though. It was the image of that man, the faithful, caring neighbor who had been there. True, he hadn't said much, but that wasn't what was important. The important fact was simply that he had been there. He had been there at the vet's office to say the final goodbye. He had been there to help dig the hole for Emma. He had been there to help bury her tired and worn-out body. And he had made the trip to our place to see yet another Emma. He had been there for this grieving couple and had walked with them through the valley of the shadow so they wouldn't have to do it alone. He hadn't been too busy or too afraid or too preoccupied with his own life to show he cared.

I was reminded of what is said to be the greatest commandment of them all, and that is to "Love thy neighbor as thyself." I had seen it fulfilled before my eyes.

Chapter 23

Our barn had an itchy problem. We had fleas! In all the years of having dogs on our place, we only had a flea problem once, but that one time quickly made up for all those easy, carefree years without them.

Here on the northeastern coast, we are usually blest with moderate weather, neither too hot nor too cold. Our winters are cold, but not too cold; and our summers can be hot, but not for very long. And evenly interspersed through it all is the welcome and needed moisture, sometimes snow, but usually rain.

There was one summer though, when the sun seemed to shine forever, day after day of temperatures in the 80's and 90's with no relief in sight and the rains failed to come. That was the year the fleas came.

Rick and I noticed that the dogs in the barn had been doing a lot of scratching for a week or so. At first we didn't think too much about it; dogs do itch, and they do scratch themselves, but this seemed to be different. Instead of an occasional itch on the belly or behind the ear, this was an incessant scratching, unlike anything we had seen before. We had never had a flea problem before so we did not immediately think of them as the possible culprit. When you aren't looking for something specific, sometimes you don't see the answer even if it's right before your eyes.

In my mind, fleas could infest other people's dogs, but not ours. I took good care of ours and kept them too clean to come down with such a nasty scourge. *Maybe the dogs are itching because their skin is dry*, I surmised. I knew mine was certainly dry so theirs could be too, I reasoned.

Then one Saturday morning after breakfast, Rick walked into the kitchen after finishing the barn chores and announced solemnly, "Guess what, Sue? We've got fleas."

I was appalled. I really didn't believe him and didn't want to believe him either, so I raced to the barn to see for myself. Shockingly, it was only too true. Crawling black miniature dots showed up plainly on the yellow dogs now that I knew what I was looking for, while they were nearly impossible to see on the two black ones.

It didn't take me long to react and act. I made a quick and rather expensive trip to the area department store where I loaded up on what I thought would take care of the problem: flea shampoo, flea powder, and flea spray. I was going all out. I figured if one remedy didn't kill the buggers, the other one would. I didn't know for sure how we had acquired this problem, but I knew I had to nip it right now before it got any worse—if it could get any worse—I might add. It seemed the longer I watched the dogs, the more fleas I saw.

I decided my first course of action would be the shampoo. Rick brought the dogs up from the barn one by one to the house where our yard hose was hooked up. It was used mainly for washing my van and Rick's and the boys' trucks, but it had another purpose now. Rick held the dogs down, or rather he attempted to hold them down, while I fiercely sprayed them with the hose to get the thick, dense fur wet. Then I poured on the foul smelling green liquid and worked up as much lather as I could with seventy to eighty pounds of solid muscle lunging this way and that, fighting against my every effort, with only one plan on their minds...escape! According to the directions on the bottle, the lather had to set for five long minutes to allow the solution to do its deadly work. Trying to force a very wet dog not to shake for five dragging minutes is quite a feat, and needless to say, we did not always succeed.

By the time we rinsed the last miserable, sodden creature off, Rick and I were drenched and wondering uneasily how many fleas had been flung on us throughout the ordeal. Although I didn't find any, I scratched for the rest of the day just thinking about it.

The dogs dried quickly in the hot sun and as soon as we could catch them again, for they warily kept their distance after their dousing, I drenched them with flea powder while Rick once more restrained them. This time when they shook, we were both plastered with white powder. I looked on the bright side and guessed that we were now protected from any fleas that might have hopped on us previously.

The instructions on the powder container said to powder the dogs' bedding as well, as the flea eggs could be embedded there even though it wasn't always possible to see any evidence of them. So I powdered and sprayed everything in the barn anywhere at all close to where the dogs slept. I did their houses, and just to make doubly sure, I powdered the sand floor in their pens too, stirring it up with my feet. This was before we had cement floors, which came years later.

I was feeling pretty good about everything. True, we had had a problem, but I felt confident we had taken care of it and it was over. Done deal!

Ha! Less than a week later, I was playing with a couple of the dogs in the yard when I spotted moving black dots on their fur again. I was appalled. After all we had done? Well, these fleas were tough, but I could be tough too, so Rick and I repeated the whole routine again; dogs, houses, and floors, hoping that this time, something would work.

Tara was due to deliver her pups any day and that made me understandably nervous. That was all I needed; tiny, defenseless, newborn pups crawling with relentless, bloodsucking fleas.

A week passed and it seemed we had beaten the enemy. The fleas were gone, and Tara had her pups, eight of them—five yellows and three blacks—in the basement birthing room. When they were about three days old, I went downstairs and idly perched on the edge of the whelping box as I watched the pups contentedly nurse. I spotted what looked like a speck of matted blood on one of the yellow pups and reached down to rub it off. Guess what? It didn't rub off, and it wasn't blood and all of a sudden it moved. Yes, it was an ugly flea. I groaned in disgust.

I quickly examined the rest of the pups and, horrors, they were all infested, along with their mother. The fleas on the yellow pups were fairly easy to spot, and I hurriedly pulled them off and squished them between my fingers, but the fleas on the black pups and their black mother were another story. I couldn't find them! I held each pup up to the luminous heat lamp and peered intently at its silky fur, ruffling it slowly with my fingers. Ah, there was one! And another!

When I felt I had defleaed the pups fairly well, I went to work on Tara. After doing my best on her, which I doubted was good enough as she is a big 80 pound dog with a lot of area to cover, I was ready to collapse.

Then a scary thought crossed my mind. If I had fleas in the basement, what was to prevent them from hopping up the stairs where we lived? Everyone knew that only dirty people got fleas, right? Not clean, decent ones. Horrors! What was I going to do? I shook my head gloomily—these poor, innocent little pups with these leeches all over them! I was livid. I decided I had only one option left, one that I really should have thought of in the first place, and that was to call my vet.

So I called and sheepishly explained my problem. What would they think? We had fleas! Cindy, the vet assistant who answered the phone, tried to make me feel better by assuring me that because of the unusually dry weather we had that year, the office was seeing one flea infestation case after another. She went on to say that there was a product on the market—yes, it seemed amazing but there was one that I had not tried—which the office recommended, that was having great results.

I explained to Cindy that it had to be safe enough to use on pregnant and nursing dogs, and then there was the added problem of the young pups too. They were only four days old.

She thought about this for a moment and then told me to come down to the office, and the doctor would talk to me.

I wasted no time in heading for Dr. Fenity's office about five miles away. After explaining the whole situation to Dr. Fenity, the kindly vet I've known ever since we took our first dog to him many years ago, he informed me of several products that had recently come on the market that would last three months with one application. The products all consisted of a liquid, which was poured directly onto the animal's skin where it was absorbed into the dog's system. It would kill fleas already on the dog, repel future fleas, and also kill any larvae that were imbedded in the fur. There were various companies that sold a form of this miracle panacea; and after reading the fine print, he found one that was absolutely safe for pregnant and nursing dogs.

But the pups were another problem. Their systems were too immature at this point to tolerate such strong medication. Even flea powder was much too harsh and concentrated. My only course of action was to comb the fleas and eggs out of their fur with a tiny fine-toothed baby comb several times each day until they disappeared or the pups got big enough to tolerate the flea powder. There was simply nothing else that could be done.

I groaned as I visualized the eight flea-covered puppies lying in my basement and all the minute fleas that would have to be combed out. I left the office loaded down with the liquid treatments for the older dogs and a small, very innocent-looking, light blue comb.

Upon arriving home, I immediately dosed Tara and the other adults. That was the easy part. Then, I set to work on the pups. I began combing the tiny, furry bodies, starting with their petite heads and ending up at their fat tails. Aha! There was one caught in the close teeth of the comb. And there was another! I was ecstatic. The yellow pups weren't too bad, at least I could see the black specks, but the black pups were another story. It was frustrating as I couldn't see what I was after, but I persisted. Many fleas later, and with eyes that now had a perpetual squint, I decided I had done what I could for the time being. I would come back later in the day and have another go at it.

As the days passed, Tara and the other adult dogs were marvelously completely rid of their tormentors—no more itching, no more crawling black dots. *That stuff really works*, I thought. But it wasn't such a success story as far as the pups were concerned. Each day I continued combing; and even though I was combing out fewer fleas than I had when I first started, they were still there. I parted and combed puppy fur week after long week, and I longed to see some light at the end of the tunnel.

The pups were getting older now, almost six weeks old, the magic age when it would be safe to powder them. But they were also getting dangerously close to the time when they would be sold, and I had a secret fear of new owners calling me on the phone and screaming in my ear that their lovely puppies had fleas, and of course, blaming me. What would this do to my reputation? I began powdering them a few days before they turned six weeks old but to my dismay, even with the ample amount of powder I was using on them, I still occasionally found a flea.

It had been almost a week since I had spotted a black dot and I began to breathe easier. It was a good thing because the pups were scheduled to leave that very weekend. I gave them one last final combing before they left and silently prayed that the bugs were really and truly gone for good. Every time the phone rang those first few days after the pups left, my stomach would churn as I imagined a new owner irately telling me that his puppy had fleas, and that no doubt it must have gotten them from my place.

Word of that going around could damage a breeder's good reputation so fast it would make your head spin. But no calls came, and I was grateful. I was also thankful that the fleas never made their appearance upstairs. Other pet owners and breeders I spoke with had not been so fortunate, and a few even ended up fumigating their entire house.

I finally had to admit it; the fleas were absolutely and completely gone, and I had learned a lot. The weather changed at last and with it the temperature cooled and the rains came once more and the dry ground disappeared. The flea epidemic across the land was over.

Today, I keep what I call the miracle flea remedy on hand year round, just in case. In the summer, whenever it stays hot and dry for any length of time, I give all of our dogs a dose of it, simply as a preventative. And I'm happy to say that we have never, ever had another problem with fleas. I am older now, and I hope a little wiser as well. I never want to relive what I went through that one frustrating year.

I have found there is a lot of truth in that old saying, 'An ounce of prevention is worth a pound of cure.' I'm a firm believer in that one.

Chapter 24

A long distance telephone call from Michigan one early morning in April changed everything. It was my mom, relaying the sad news that my uncle had passed away during the night. When my aunt had awakened in the morning and noticed that her husband was not yet up, she had gone to awaken him only to find that she could not. Indeed, he would never wake again.

To be sure, Uncle Gary had been sickly for many years, but still his death came as a surprise. No one in the family had been expecting this to happen any time soon. And, it does seem that no one ever really does plan on dying, even though deep down we all know that one day we must.

It reminds me of my husband's Great-Aunt Gert, who at ninety-five is still enjoying fairly good health. She told me she had a riddle that she needed an answer to: "I don't want to live forever," she said, "but I don't want to die tomorrow either. What is the solution?"

That's a good question, and I certainly didn't have the answer, but I suppose it's a question that we really don't *have* to answer as the power of life and death are rarely in our hands and we are probably better off not knowing some things, especially the things that are beyond our control.

It is no secret that my uncle's wife, my Aunt Carol Jean, has always been my favorite aunt. She has catered to my whims ever since I was a small girl, making me mouth-watering cherry pies when she realized they were my favorite and explaining to me the mysteries of candy making. Together, we made chocolate fudge, white pecan divinity and chewy caramels wrapped in wax paper at Christmas time and taco salad in the summer. She is a wonderful cook and is always game to try something new.

My aunt is a small woman whose round, cheerful face always welcomed me with undisguised pleasure, and her home was almost as familiar to me as my own. Her children, my three cousins, and I had loads of fun in the hot summers playing freeze tag and hide-and-go-seek and in the winter, skating together on the creek and in the shallow ditch in front of our house. I seldom saw any of them anymore as many miles, three states, and a province separated us. However, on our family's yearly trips home, I always made it a priority to stop in at Aunt Carol Jean's for a catch-me-up visit. Like as not, she'd send me away with some of her latest baking efforts.

I had more memories tied up with her than I could count, and I desperately wanted to go to my uncle's funeral. She had done so much for me in years past and I wanted to do this for her now.

Well go then, I told myself, but it wasn't that easy. Part of the problem, as usual, was the dogs. Normally, I only have one litter of pups at a time, but this time I had two litters. They had been born a day apart, with a grand total of eighteen pups. Those were a hectic two days when they had all been born.

I can remember wishing we had an escalator from the kitchen to the basement where the birthing room was located. All I did for two days and nights was go upstairs and downstairs, upstairs and downstairs. Thank goodness for the local pizza shop a mile away and an easygoing family that loves pancakes and grilled cheese sandwiches. After helping deliver eighteen pups, the last thing I felt like doing was cooking.

Licorice and her five pups stayed down in the basement room, and Meg and her thirteen pups went to the heated room in the barn where there was more space. Eventually, all of them would be in the barn together.

Needless to say, I was kept busy, especially as the pups grew older. When they are little, the moms do all the work. As they get bigger, I do all the work, the feeding and the cleaning, especially the cleaning; and cleaning up after eighteen puppies is nothing to sneeze at.

If I was going to Uncle Gary's funeral, I would have to leave the next day, and there were three obstacles looming in front of me. The first was getting an affordable airline ticket on such short notice. Driving 700 miles alone was definitely not an option. The second was finding someone to get my two younger sons on to the bus in the morning and to be waiting for them when they returned home in the afternoon. The third one was getting the six-week old pups to the vet for their first shots and physicals, an appointment that was scheduled for the day of my uncle's funeral.

Under ordinary circumstances, I would have simply canceled the appointment and rescheduled for a later time, but eighteen pups at one time were not considered normal circumstances, and this appointment absolutely could not be canceled. As can be imagined, the appointment for all these pups had been made long ago and occupied a sizable time slot at the veterinarian's office. It wouldn't be fair to my vet to cancel out with all this time saved just for me; and even if I did cancel, it would be impossible to get another appointment later in the week with the amount of time needed for eighteen pups. This was a one-man office, and he was booked solid weeks in advance. Besides, I really did need the pups to be seen now, as they would be leaving for new homes in a week or so. They needed shots given and physical exam forms filled out before they left.

I knew what my heart wanted to do, but how would I arrange for everything to be handled? So many things seemed to be out of my hands. So I prayed throughout the day that if I was supposed to go to this funeral, the right doors would be opened for me; and if I was not supposed to go, the doors would remain closed. Now I could relax. It was out of my hands.

I told my mother-in-law about my dilemma and she readily agreed to come over in the mornings to make the boys' lunches and see them to the bus. And then Rick decided that, although he was very busy at work right then, he could still manage to leave early enough in order to be home for the kids. He would also take care of feeding and cleaning the pups each day that I was gone. That solved one problem.

Then I called my faithful friend Pat, who has been there for me through thick and thin throughout the years and has bailed me out of countless predicaments. I told her about my puppy problem, and without a moment's hesitation, she volunteered to take all eighteen pups to the vet for me. Now that's what you call a good friend!

Pat is a spunky lady who is an animal lover through and through. Over the years, she has raised and taken care of Dobermans, raccoons, llamas, peacocks, deer, turkeys, bottle-fed lambs; you name it, and she's had it in her living room at one time or another. One more problem solved.

I still had to get a ticket, so I called the airline I usually traveled on. I was right. The price was astronomical at this short notice. Then my sister from Indiana called. She had a friend who was a travel agent and my sister was able to persuade her to get on her computer at home to find me an affordable ticket. The agent found a jet leaving from my airport here on the east coast that would get me to Cleveland. There I would change airlines and take a small propeller plane to a tiny airport in Michigan about 100 miles from my parents' home.

My sister would pick me up there on her way up from Indiana, and we would drive together to my parents' home. On the way back, she would do the same. The best part was that the ticket was unbelievably reasonable for being so last minute, and the clincher was that there was only one left. It was as if it had my name on it. I took it. The doors had opened wide. I was supposed to go.

I spent the rest of the evening packing and writing numerous lists of instructions, which I needn't have bothered with as I've found that no one ever reads them anyway. I called Pat to let her know I had lined up Linda, another friend of mine, who would go with her to the vet's office to help with the pups. I felt eighteen lively bodies would be a little much even for Superwoman herself to handle. The next morning, Rick drove me to the airport and I was off, bag and baggage, leaving my cares and responsibilities behind. It was a good feeling, knowing that everything was being taken care of while I was gone. I wasn't as indispensable as I thought, and I would only be gone for three days.

Everything went as planned. My sister, whom I hadn't seen in ages, picked me up at the airport in Michigan and we had a great time talking about all the things that sisters usually talk about as we drove.

That evening as I walked into the funeral home and saw the simultaneous expressions of astonishment and then gratefulness in my aunt's eyes, it made it all worthwhile. She could scarcely believe that I would travel all those miles for her. As she hugged me tight, I realized it was a blessing I could do this for myself as well. I was so thankful I had made the effort to come. I knew without a doubt that I had done the right thing.

The days passed too fast and soon I was home again. The kids had made out just fine in the mornings with Grandma. I walked down to the barn, and the pups looked great. Everyone seemed to have gotten along just fine without me.

I noticed the vet forms lying on the dining room table, so I assumed the pups had gone to the vet as planned. I decided to give Pat a call and get the scoop on how things had gone. She had plenty to say. She had quite the experience, one that she would certainly remember—she assured me—for a long time.

"The morning started out good enough," Pat reflected, "but it was awfully hot and sticky, unusual weather for May. Linda met me outside the barn, and we started carrying pups out and putting them into the back of the truck."

I had previously volunteered our van, but Pat had said her pickup truck would be fine. She had a cap over the bed and this was where the pups were placed.

"What did you put them in, in the truck I mean?" I asked curiously. I always found that putting the pups into wash baskets seemed to work the best for me. The baskets kept them in one place during the ride and made it easy to carry them into the office.

She sighed. "We didn't put them in anything; we just put them in the back of the truck. It would have been all right," she continued, "but I had forgotten that there were still leaves and lawn trimmings in the back from raking the yard a month ago. The pups ran around like crazy in there, rolling over each other, leaves flying all over the place, but that was okay."

She hesitated for a moment. "And, it still would have been okay except it was so beastly hot and muggy. It had to be in the nineties and the air was so still and heavy. Linda was worried that they would need water during the ride to the vet's so she filled a few dishes with water and put them in the back with the pups. What a disaster!" Pat exclaimed, sighing. "By the time I pulled in at the vet's office, all of the water had spilled out, and the pups were covered with mud. Then add the half-rotten decaying leaves to it and you've got a blooming mess! And, I think a couple of them must have gone to the bathroom on the way too," she muttered. "It was horrendous!"

I could hear the exasperation in her normally cool, collected voice. "Sue, you wouldn't have believed it," she insisted. "I was so embarrassed to take those filthy puppies into that office."

"What did you do?" I asked in stunned disbelief.

"What could we do?" she asked, exasperation flooding her voice. "We carried all the pups in and put them in a room and closed the door. Then they ran circles around each other until the doctor came in."

I closed my eyes, visualizing the mad scene. When I visited the office, I always kept the pups confined to the wash baskets. It was so calm and orderly.

She went on. "After each pup was checked and given its shot, Linda or I would carry it back to the truck where we popped it in the back again." She sighed again, remembering. "Sue, you just can't imagine the smell."

She was wrong there. I'm sure I could—only too clearly.

Whatever had my vet and his assistants thought? I wondered.

Changing the subject a little, I asked, "How did the pups check out, Pat? Any problems?" Once in a while I had a slight hernia or an overbite or a heart murmur, usually nothing too serious.

"Oh, they checked out just fine," she confirmed. "No problems at all."

Well, that was good news at least.

"What a day though!" she admitted.

Yes, I could see that she had had quite a day, quite an experience, but I also knew my friend Pat. I hadn't known her for fifteen years for nothing. I knew that if I were in a bind, I could ask her tomorrow to do the same thing for me, and she would do it without batting an eye, without thinking twice, although I was sure she would persuade Linda to leave the water pans at home if there really was a next time. She was a true blue friend.

"I owe you big time, Pat," I said, "and Linda too," I added. And I really did. How many people would agree to take eighteen six-week-old squirming pups to the vet without a murmur? And, Pat's truck must have been a royal mess to clean up, but not one word of complaint did I hear from her about that.

In spite of everything, my two friends had come through for me. They had carried every wriggling, dirty pup into the office and back out again. I can only imagine what their clothes looked and smelled like when they got home. Not only did they finish an enormous job, they made it possible for me to take a trip that meant so much to me and, I believe, to my dear aunt too. Yes, a friend in need is a friend indeed. Indeed.

Chapter 25

Some dogs are real people lovers. The more people around them giving them attention, the happier they are. Then there are dogs who will only bond with their human families, while others give their heart to only one person. These dogs tend to be very possessive and protective of their humans which has its good points and bad. This is the story of Meg, our one person dog. Rick and I had long planned a trip to Michigan to visit relatives which should have posed no problem except Meg was about to have puppies.

Meg is our sweetest and most sensitive dog. Her dark eyes radiate compassion and gentleness. She has so many good attributes that she is, hands down, one of my favorite dogs. However, she is also the most timid and people-shy dog we own. She is easily frightened and tends to be clingy. For some strange reason, it is extremely difficult for her to trust people. She won't even allow someone outside the family to pet her.

While most Labs are known for their outgoing, sociable natures, Meg is a one-person dog, and that person happens to be me. I suppose it's only natural as I am the one who spends the most time with her. I am the one who is with her when her pups are born and who takes her for walks and spoils her by allowing her in the house for no special reason. She tolerates the rest of our family but everyone knows who really rates.

When we go for walks, she is constantly rubbing her soft head up against me and nuzzling my hands. She can scarcely bear to have me out of her sight. While out on our jaunts, she'll sometimes run ahead to inspect something that's aroused her curiosity, but she'll only stay away for a minute or two. Then with nervous, darting eyes, she'll race back, tail wagging like crazy, to make sure I'm still there, that I haven't disappeared into thin air or something. It's rather ego boosting to know that someone absolutely adores you, that you can do no wrong in their eyes, and that they can scarcely stand to be apart from you, even though that someone happens to be a dog. But sometimes it can be a bit too much, and in some instances, it can even be a problem.

Anyway, the trip to Michigan had been carefully planned for some time. Unfortunately, it would be very close to the time when Megs pups were due. I was tired of forever trying to work our plans around the dogs, so this time I had made up my mind that we were going, regardless of anyone or anything. To be sure, we rarely leave our place for long as the dogs do tend to tie us down. They are a big responsibility, and Rick and I do take it seriously. However, once in a while, it's just nice to go away when you want, without taking into consideration whether it's convenient for the dogs or not.

So we were going. Our minds were made up and I reminded myself that it wasn't as if Meg was a first-time mother. She had delivered several fine litters over the years with no birthing problems and she wasn't actually due until the day before we were scheduled to return. And in spite of the fact that our dogs usually whelp very close to, or exactly on, their due dates, there was a chance that she would still be waiting with a big belly when we returned from our trip on Saturday.

I consoled myself with the fact that Doug, our nineteen-year-old son, would be home to keep an eye on her and would look in on her several times a day in the basement birthing room where she would be staying, just in case.

I had extra reassurance about the situation because on Friday, the day that she was actually due, even if things were still quiet and calm, Doug would load Meg up in our dog crate and deliver her to my good friend Pat's house, where she would keep an eagle eye on her until we returned. I had the utmost confidence in Pat. She was an animal person to the *nth* degree, and there wasn't much that she couldn't handle.

So I packed and Rick loaded our faithful old red van and after a few last-minute instructions to Doug and a couple of hurried phone calls to Pat, we were off. I felt pretty optimistic about leaving Meg, but I was not totally at ease because I knew Meg and her quirky personality. I knew she would be fine with Doug because he was one of the family, but Pat wasn't and that could be a bit of a problem.

The week passed and every day I would call home and interrogate Doug. Was Meg acting normal? Was she panting? Was she still eating? I knew from experience that a usually ever-hungry expectant mom suddenly refusing food was a sure sign of impending labor. Doug allayed my fears and assured me each day that she was doing just fine. He was feeding her, giving her water, and letting her out every day for a little exercise. She was fine, he assured me again.

Friday, the day before we were to leave for home, the phone rang in the early afternoon. It was Pat, and she was frantic. As planned, Doug had taken Meg and her crate over that morning and had deposited them in Pat's warm basement. He told her that Meg had refused her food that morning, and Pat had made the correct assumption that the pups were most likely on their way. And sure enough, three healthy yellow puppies had promptly been born, but there was a slight problem.

Pat had done her best to coax Meg out of the crate after Doug left so she could be more comfortable, but Meg had a stubborn mind of her own. She growled and showed her teeth. The fur on her back stood up, issuing a very real warning. Pat was afraid, and rightly so, to just pull her out. Meg anchored herself firmly and simply refused to leave that crate so the three pups had been born on the floor of the large metal crate. Needless to say, Pat could not get anywhere near them.

I clenched the phone tightly in my hands, visualizing the whole scene as Pat talked on. She was upset, and I didn't blame her. I was upset myself. I could hear the emotion in her voice as she described the situation. "Sue, I can't even tell if they're males or females unless they roll onto their backs," she lamented. "If I come anywhere near that crate, Meg growls and acts as if she'd like to take my head off. I have to hide around the corner of the room and sneak looks at the pups. It's a good thing they all seem to be healthy," she added.

"Are they nursing?" I asked quickly. Pat knew as well as I did how vitally important it is that newborns nurse as soon after birth as possible.

"Thank goodness they are," she declared. "But if they weren't, there's not one thing I'd be able to do about it, with that mom the way she is."

Yes, thank goodness, I thought. I knew how hard this had to be on Pat. She was one of those people who liked to be in the very middle of things. I knew it was killing her not to be able to inspect and cuddle those pups. She was scarcely able to get a decent look at them, let alone touch them.

"Can you somehow give Meg some water and food?" I asked. "She must be awfully thirsty after being in labor all morning. And she'll need food to keep her strength up so she can nurse those pups."

"Well, I did manage to sneak in a bowl of water and a dish of dog food when she was turned the other way, cleaning up a pup. As soon as she saw me though, she growled and lunged at me.

"Sue, I don't doubt for a minute that she'd bite me if she had half a chance," Pat said, thoroughly discouraged. "And, you know what else?" she went on worriedly, "I don't know how I'm going to get her out of that crate so she can go to the bathroom. I know she has to go; she hasn't gone since Doug brought her here this morning, and now it's 4:00 o'clock. Every time I go near her, she crouches and growls, and I think she means business," she ended knowingly.

"Well," I said encouragingly, "If she has to go bad enough, she'll go out for you. The last thing she wants to do is make a mess in her crate with those puppies in there."

Dogs are clean creatures by nature, and they will try their hardest to keep the area closest to them clean and free of waste. Only if there is no other recourse will a dog mess in its crate, its temporary home.

"Well, let's hope so," Pat said rather doubtfully.

"By the way, what time do you expect to be home tomorrow?"

I sighed and looked at the clock. We were 700 miles away, and it took twelve straight hours of fast, detour-free, bathroom-and-gas stop only, driving. I felt like leaving right then, but I knew that was impossible. We had too many loose ends to wrap up before we could pull out.

"We plan on leaving at 4:00 in the morning so we should be home roughly around 4:00 p.m. Then count on another hour until we get to your house. Probably around 5:00 I guess." I just hoped those pups would keep nursing and that somehow Meg would relent and allow Pat to take her outside so she could relieve herself.

Most dogs, Meg included, instinctively eat the afterbirth and other fetal membranes that are delivered along with their pups. There are two possible theories why. One is that in the wild, animal mothers instinctively clean up all evidence of a birth so predators are not alerted by the smell and thus drawn in. Another theory is that the placenta contains maternal antibodies that are important for the health of the pups and when a mom eats these, she is in essence passing on her inherent immunities to her babies. I'm not sure which of these is true, but it really doesn't matter. What I did know for a fact, though, and what did matter was that after eating several afterbirths, the mom almost always developed a serious case of diarrhea, and I do mean serious. If Meg continued to refuse to leave her crate, it could be a real mess for Pat. I couldn't wait to get home. I fervently wished once more that I wasn't 700 miles away.

It took me quite a while to fall asleep that night. My thoughts were 700 miles away and then suddenly I was rudely awakened by the shrill ringing of the alarm clock in the still dark morning. The clock dial read 3:45. It was time we were on our way. After a flurry of hurried hugs and good-byes, Rick backed the loaded van out of the driveway, and we were off. The day passed slowly, and my thoughts kept returning to my girl Meg. Poor dog, she was probably scared to death without me, sensitive thing that she was. Thank goodness we made good time on the highway.

After what seemed like a very long day, we finally made the familiar turn into our driveway. I quickly unpacked the things that had to be taken into the house, and then Rick and I set off for Pat's, wondering what we would find.

Pulling into Pat's driveway, I jumped out of the van almost before Rick stopped it. Instead of going to the back door as I usually did, I decided to save time by running down the wooden outside steps that led to the basement and Meg. I flung open the walkout door, and there she was, or rather I should say, there they were, my sweet gal Meg and her three golden babies.

Pat was standing off to the side with an exasperated look on her face and furiously shook her head when I asked if Meg had left the crate yet. I was quickly counting in my head—it couldn't be—but it was! It had been almost thirty-five hours since she had been outside, yet the crate was dry and clean. There was no evidence at all of puppies being born besides the actual pups themselves. She had cleaned everything up as usual.

As soon as Meg saw me, her tail started wagging nonstop and she fixed me with weary, but still gentle eyes that clearly said only one thing, *I knew you would come, I was waiting* for you. She would never think of blaming me for not being there when she needed me most. Instead, she had simply made up her mind to wait for me, and wait she did. She trusted me completely.

Am I really worthy of such absolute trust? I asked myself.

I motioned Pat to stay towards the back of the room so Meg couldn't see her. Then I unlatched the crate door and bent over so my head was nearly in the crate.

"Come on, Meggie," I entreated softly. "Let's go outside." She stared at me and then at her pups, hesitating as if trying to make up her mind. "Come on, girl, let's go," I begged once more. She rose slowly and, in no hurry at all, gave her pups a final departing sniff and stepped out. She looked up at me and paused for a moment as she glanced back at her babies once more and then at me. I knew what she was thinking.

"They'll be okay, girl," I assured her as I petted her soft fur. "I promise you."

She gave me one more look, a look that spoke volumes. It said very plainly, *I've always believed you, and I believe you now.* It was a look of complete confidence and I was truly humbled. I swallowed the lump in my throat, and together we went through the door and walked outside into the bright sunshine. I hoped I would always be deserving of such a trust.

Chapter 26

If only they could speak! How many times I have wished that my lovable Labs could communicate, really communicate with me! Oh, sure, I can usually figure out most things after a while, but there are times when a lot of guessing occurs on their part as well as mine.

For instance, when one of our barn dogs begins to howl in the middle of the night for no reason at all as far as I'm concerned, it would be so great to be able to simply holler out the window, "Now tell me, exactly why are you barking? Do you see something or hear something that I should know about?" and get a definite answer.

And, yes, it would surely be helpful to be able to ask our moms during labor and delivery, "Have all your puppies been born? Can I go back to bed or is there still one more that I should wait up for?" and get a plain yes or no answer instead of frustrated second guessing.

There are certainly times when a little extra information would be greatly appreciated and beneficial.

It was the middle of March; and after enduring a particularly cold and snowy New England winter, Rick and I had just returned from a week's relaxing vacation down South. My parents had made the trip from Michigan to care for our children while we were gone, so we had really and truly relaxed. In fact, the heaviest decision we had to make all week was what to order for dinner each night—bliss indeed. My battery was fully recharged and I felt ready to take on life again.

We returned home on a Wednesday night around 10:30 and the first thing I spotted was a row of messages tacked to the bulletin board. One in particular caught my eye. "Call Naomi when you get home," my mom had written, and then underneath the phone number she had added ominously, "She bought a pup from you in January and he is biting people."

"Oh no," I groaned. "That doesn't sound good," I continued to read down the list of messages. Two notes down from the "Naomi" message was another one. "Call Naomi when you get home. She is having problems with her dog."

"Naomi," I said out loud as I shook my head. I couldn't place her, but that really wasn't unusual. There had been two good-sized litters that left around the same time in January, and my memory was awful. I glanced at the clock again. Thank goodness it was too late to call tonight.

Nothing like getting hit the minute you walk in the door, I thought to myself. Relaxing vacation memories were dissipating rather too quickly for my liking. But, yes, the vacation really was over and this was part of the real life.

After a long night of tossing and turning with my thoughts ever returning to the problem that needed to be dealt with in the morning, I wearily climbed out of bed. While it was true that I always encouraged customers to call me with any questions they had and to keep me informed of any problems they encountered with their pups, deep down I must admit that I truly hoped no one would ever call. Sometimes I got a little weary being a telephone counselor and trainer, always at the beck and call of new owners. But actually, few people did call. Time seemed to resolve a lot of problems, thank goodness. But there were times when the problems were very real and definitely needed to be dealt with, and I would be a poor excuse of a breeder if I ignored them.

As soon as our boys left for school and work, and the house was quiet again, I decided to make the call to Naomi. *Might as well get it over with,* I reasoned, *instead of making myself miserable thinking about it.* I dialed the number. The thought went through my head that perhaps she wouldn't be home and I could still put it off a bit. But Naomi was home, and yes, she did indeed have a problem. She had lots to tell me, so I merely listened for about fifteen minutes, once in a while interjecting a question.

And then it hit me; I remembered who she was. She was the sweet, soft-spoken, grandmotherly looking woman who had come with her husband to buy my last pup, a perky black male. I remembered now that she had told me that they hadn't had a dog for thirty years, and she was very concerned about wanting to do all the right things with this pup. I had assured her at the time that a good dose of common sense and a firm hand were probably all she would need. After all, Labs had wonderful reputations for their willing and friendly natures, I had reminded her.

Something had gone very wrong though, and I was puzzled. Jacob, her puppy, was four months old and had started this odd biting behavior about a month earlier.

"He bites anything and everyone," she explained in a puzzled, patient tone of voice. "My arms and hands are covered with bite marks as well as my legs. It's like he can't control himself."

I closed my eyes for a moment as my mind made a rapid mental picture of the sweet grandmother I remembered, her body covered with angry, red bite marks. It was not a pleasant picture.

She went on, "I've tried all kinds of things to make him stop, and he does settle down at times, but soon he's right back to the same thing." I heard her sigh, and then she continued. "He won't listen to 'no' anymore; in fact, it seems to make him angry when I do say it."

This raised a red flag in my mind; a four-month-old Lab pup should not even have a concept of anger.

Naomi went on. "Someone told me to try holding his mouth shut with my hands when he gets like this, but that doesn't work either. It just seems to frustrate him. I've tried swatting him with a rolled up newspaper. You know, I don't want to hurt him, but nothing seems to work. Another thing that bothers me terribly," she continued, "is that Jacob's not affectionate."

"What do you mean?" I queried. Everyone knows that Labs crave attention and usually tend to give back even more affection than they receive.

"Well, I've been trying to teach him how to give kisses, to be affectionate, but he absolutely refuses. He won't cuddle or nuzzle me either," she said in a sad tone of voice. "I thought Labs were supposed to be so loving."

"They are, usually," I answered, and it was true. In fact, some of our dogs are almost too mushy; I'm always pushing them away from me. It seems they can never get close enough to you.

My mind was racing, trying to make some sense of all the things Naomi had told me and to come up with a wise answer, but my mind was blank. I did know one thing though, and that was that this was definitely not normal behavior. I knew Naomi was home most of the time so the dog was not lacking for attention. There were no small children around the house that perhaps might be teasing him, making him belligerent. My thoughts were interrupted by Naomi.

"I've even tried to reward him with doggie treats when he comes close to my face. Other people's dogs give them kisses, but Jacob just won't." I could hear the intense feeling of rejection in her voice. She was giving her all, but she was being refused.

"I've tried so many different things," she said tiredly. "When he starts these biting fits, I try to distract him by rubbing his tummy or playing ball with him, and he's fine as long as it lasts, but the minute I stop...." Her voice trailed off, and I knew what happened. "I've tried everyone's advice on how to discipline him. You know we haven't had a dog for so long, maybe we just don't know what we're doing anymore."

"Nonsense," I said in what I hoped was an encouraging tone of voice. I desperately tried to think of some sage words of wisdom to give her, but I was coming up empty. I really was at a complete loss as to how I could help her. "You're doing all the right things," I assured her. "Perhaps...." and here I hesitated. I didn't want to even think it, but it was remotely possible I supposed. "Perhaps, it's just the dog. Maybe there's just something mentally deficient in him." I swallowed hard after saying that, but you never did know. Those kinds of things happened to people, so why not animals? I did know, however, that this problem was definitely not a hereditary one. There was no calmer or more lovable dog than Lion, the pup's sire, and Tara, his mom, was a peach too.

"Well, we're not giving up yet," the ever-patient Naomi answered in her soft voice. "I have an appointment tomorrow with a personal trainer, a dog trainer, that is. Maybe she'll have an idea of what's going on."

Bless her, I thought. She was going the extra mile; she was definitely not a quitter!

"That's an excellent idea!" I exclaimed. "What we need is an expert who has dealt with all kinds of dog problems, in short, someone who can think like a dog."

I was relieved. Maybe this trainer would have some answers. I knew I certainly didn't have any. I had dealt with many types of behavior issues in the past, but this was a new one for me.

"Naomi, please keep me posted on this," I implored.

"I want to know what happens. This definitely shouldn't have to be your problem alone, and I will work with you until we get to the bottom of it," I promised.

"Oh, I will," she assured me. "Don't worry."

But I was worrying. I felt terrible that I really hadn't been able to help her. The weekend passed and I wondered how the meeting with the trainer had gone. What was the verdict? Was this pup of mine a hopeless, demented case? Was he beyond help? Would he have to be put down? I shuddered to even think of that possibility.

I didn't have long to wonder, for early Monday morning, Naomi called. "Sue, I just have to tell you what happened," she said in an excited, breathless voice. "You're just never going to believe it!"

I steeled myself for the worst.

"It's like night and day!" she went on.

I was all ears, my curiosity at the breaking point.

"Oh, no, what happened?" I asked nervously.

"Well, first of all, the trainer was a really nice woman. She told me she's been training dogs for quite a few years," Naomi informed me. "And the very first thing she did when I brought Jacob into the room to meet her was to check him all over real good, you know, examine him."

Okay, I thought to myself; *now get ready. What did she find?*

"You'll never believe it," she repeated. "The trainer looked in his mouth and found that his gums were terribly swollen. In fact, she said that if a baby had gums as swollen as Jacob's, it would be crying twenty-four hours a day." She paused for a moment and then added. "She said he had to be in dreadful pain."

"No," I breathed in disbelief and unabashed relief.

Something so simple! Why hadn't I thought of that? But then I knew that most puppies exhibit little or no outward sign when their teeth come in. This was a very unusual case. Jacob had been trying the only way he knew how to communicate his pain, and neither of us had picked up on it. I understood now. My dog wasn't crazy after all; he was just hurting so badly that it made him lash out at everything and everyone. Something as simple as his permanent adult teeth pushing through had turned a small puppy into a monster.

"What else did she say?" I pressed eagerly.

"Well, she said to feed him ice cubes and frozen carrots, as many as he wanted, to help numb the soreness. And we did. He just loves them," she giggled girlishly. "It's just like night and day!" she repeated incredulously. "It really works!" she exclaimed, and her soft voice had a triumphant ring to it.

Why, yes, that made perfect sense, now that I thought of it. When our boys were babies and had been fussy—which was often—I had given them water-filled teething rings that I had frozen to soothe their inflamed gums.

Naomi continued, "The trainer also showed me how to massage Jacob's gums with my fingers; and you know, he just loves it! In fact, he hardly lets me stop."

I could hear the exultation in her voice and I was *so, so* happy, as much for her as for myself.

"You know," she went on, "it's only been three days since we've been doing these things and already he's so much calmer, so much more contented."

I could just imagine. "Why Naomi, that's simply wonderful," I managed to say. *If only we had known earlier,* I couldn't help but think. *How much pain and frustration could have been avoided by everyone!*

However, our animal friends can't speak to us, so it's up to us to read between the lines, to read the body language, and to decide what certain actions really mean. And sometimes we fail. Sometimes we mess up. Sometimes we just can't figure things out. How grateful I was for this intuitive trainer who could think...yes, think like a dog.

My train of thought was broken by Naomi once more.

"And do you know what else, Sue?" Naomi asked shyly. Her voice was so soft I had to listen carefully.

"What?" I asked, wondering what else she had to tell me.

"Jacob even gave me a kiss yesterday!"

Chapter 27

People choose a dog for lots of different reasons. Many times someone will buy a puppy from me as a special gift for someone they love. Boyfriends buy pups for their girlfriends and vice versa. Wives buy pups for their husbands and vice versa. Parents buy pups for their children. The list goes on and on. Sometimes people will buy a dog to make a special occasion even more memorable. There have been pups bought for birthdays, graduations, anniversaries, Mother's and Father's Day, Valentine's Day and Christmas presents. I've only sold one puppy, though, that was bought by an entire office. An office full of people who cared about someone very deeply, someone who was extremely special to all of them, and this is that story. It's the extraordinary story of very ordinary people, people who weren't afraid to care and show that they cared.

I remember that it was at the tail end of a litter of pups when I received the call. I had one male and one female left, and I was eagerly looking forward to having some time for myself again. Don't get me wrong, I wholeheartedly enjoy the pups. But after two months of being the midwife, maid, cleaning lady and food-delivery person, I was ready for a much needed break.

It was a cool morning in the fall when I received the call. An anxious voice greeted me asking the very familiar question, "I was wondering, I mean *we* were wondering, if you have any puppies left for sale?"

"Yes," I replied reassuringly. "I do have two pups left, one male and one female."

"Oh, you do?" the feminine voice breathed a sigh of relief. "Could you save the girl for us? That's the one all of us want," she said firmly.

All of us? Did I hear her right? Is that what she said? I wondered. "Well," I answered hesitantly and I frowned slightly.

"I really can't hold the pup for you without a deposit. I've done this in the past, and then the person sometimes doesn't show up and in the meantime, I've turned away other would-be buyers. If you're seriously interested, I'd strongly encourage you to come down as soon as possible, especially as I have only the one female left," I added.

"Oh, I don't know," the voice sounded a bit doubtful. "You see there's a bunch of us buying the puppy. It might take us a couple days to all get together and collect the money." She added apprehensively, "I'd sure hate for it to be gone by the time some of us could come out though."

"You're not getting the pup for yourself?" I inquired curiously.

"No, no I'm not." Then she proceeded to explain.

"See, there's this guy at work, his name is Bruce and he's got cancer. He did have cancer anyway. We're hoping it's gone now, but we're not sure, of course.

"Anyway, he's, well, he's changed. He's awfully weak from the surgery and all the treatments he's gone through, and he's gotten really discouraged." She took a deep breath and went on. "A bunch of us at work decided he needed something to get up for in the morning, something that would lift his spirits and make him want to live," she said earnestly, "and then we got this idea of getting him a puppy. He lives at home with his mother since he's gotten sick. She's all for this too," she hastened to add. "She'd help take care of it, so you wouldn't have to worry about that," she ended a bit breathlessly.

I had been silently thinking while my caller had been talking, and I had come to an easy decision. These were special circumstances, and under special circumstances, you made special rules and did special things.

"What a thoughtful thing to do," I said, marveling at the good friends Bruce had. "I don't usually do this, but I think I could manage to hold the pup for you for a few days anyway."

"That would be super!" she exclaimed, undisguised relief flooding her voice. "You see, we're all doing this because Bruce is such a swell guy, and we've all known him for such a long time. He used to be a real joker," she went on. "He used to be the life of the party, but now he's, well, he's gotten really quiet; he's changed somehow," she repeated uneasily. "It bothers us, the way he is, and a bunch of us decided we wanted to do something to help, something that would maybe help him get back to the way he used to be," she said wistfully.

Who says the world is a cold, uncaring place? I thought to myself.

There are still people out there who genuinely care about each other and not only say they care, but are willing to do something, to go the extra mile to show they care. There is a difference, I mused.

We talked a bit more and agreed that I would save the pup for her until the next Thursday, when she and some others from work would drive out and take the puppy home with them.

On Thursday I spent extra time with the protesting, wriggling pup, determined to have her looking especially nice. After all, this pup had an extra-special mission to perform. I scrubbed her dingy black coat in the deep stainless steel sink and rinsed and dried her with my own blow dryer upstairs. I sprinkled her now glossy fur with some of my own lilac bath powder. I so wanted her to make a good impression.

"Listen here," I said out loud to the soft ball of energy I was firmly holding in my arms. "You have a job to do. You have to be on your best behavior and try to help Bruce get well again. You can't act wild and race around, you know."

The pup looked up at me, its shiny, intelligent, dark eyes meeting mine, seemingly taking it all in.

It was late morning when a car slowly drove up the driveway and stopped next to the house. I watched out the window as the car doors opened and two young women and a middle-aged one stepped out. They went around to the back door and very carefully helped a tall, very thin, frail-looking young man about thirty or so swing first one foot and then the other, and finally his body, out of the car.

That must be Bruce, I surmised. His face had an understandably tired look on it, but it also had an uncertain, doubtful look on it too, as if he wasn't at all sure about this whole thing. I noticed he was wearing a bright red baseball cap that was in severe contrast to his pale, wan face. It was most likely covering a newly bald head, I guessed.

One of the young women and the older woman, whom I supposed was his mother, each took one of his arms and slowly but gently guided him up the few steps to our back door.

I quickly opened the door and welcomed them in and hurriedly pulled a chair out for Bruce as it was plain to see how very weak he really was. They had been driving for an hour and a half and the trip had tired him, even though the women assured me that he had been lying down in the backseat the entire way.

The women introduced themselves, and as I had thought, the weary, but patient-looking, older woman was Bruce's mother, and one of the other women was Dawn, who had been the caller I had spoken at length with a few days before. The remaining woman was Sandy, a friend and one of the many co-workers who was making this pup a reality.

I walked into the dining room where the pup was sitting quietly in her crate. I lifted the latch and swung open the door and lifted the sweet-smelling pup out and brought her into the living room where everyone was seated and waiting expectantly. All was quiet for a long moment.

Then the women started oohing and aahing and exclaiming over the curious, wide-eyed, chubby pup but Bruce didn't say a word. He just gazed tiredly at her, perhaps wondering how he would ever manage to care for her.

I walked over and placed the pup on Bruce's narrow lap, and instead of squirming and jumping around like most puppies do at this young age, she looked around a bit and sniffed his pants before simply laying her head down on her outstretched paws and calmly going to sleep.

I was amazed. *Perhaps,* I thought, *it was the bath that had tired her out, but it seemed as if she knew that Bruce needed her to be quiet and still. Was that possible?*

At first, Bruce touched the pup a bit awkwardly, almost self-consciously, but in a few minutes he began confidently stroking the sleek fur, and soon he was rubbing her ears gently with his long, tapered fingers.

I watched quietly as a contented look stole across his wan features, and for the first time since coming through the door, he smiled. We talked a little more about what to expect with a new puppy and about her care and so on. Bruce's mom promised to do all she could to help, and I knew immediately that she was the sort of person who could, and would, aptly take charge of any situation.

They had a lengthy trip back home ahead of them yet, and Bruce obviously needed his rest, so it wasn't long before they decided it was time for them to start back.

After a few final words, they made their way to the door. Bruce's mom and Sandy patiently helped him on with his coat, and each gave him an arm to cling to as they slowly walked out, while Dawn carried the now wide-awake pup that was sniffing her ear intently.

Just before she walked out the door, Dawn came over to where I was standing and whispered quietly, "Don't worry about the puppy, Susan. If something happens to Bruce, well, his mom or one of us will take care of her. She will be loved, I promise you," she assured me as her unfaltering eyes met my own.

And I knew she would.

Then they were gone, and the car with its doubly precious cargo rolled out of the driveway. I waved from the porch until the car disappeared from view.

That little pup, what will they name her? I wondered dream-ily. And then it hit me. I thought of the perfect name. Hope. I would have named her Hope...hope that better days lay ahead...hope that Bruce would make a full recovery...hope that life would get back to the way it once was for him. *What would the world be without hope?* I mused. What would people be like if, when everything went to pieces around them, they didn't have hope to go on?

I was suddenly seized with a deep appreciation for all the things that were so precious to me, my loving family, my cozy home, and most of all, the gift of good health which is priceless indeed.

I looked around at the blue fall sky, at the lofty trees bordering our yard that were starting to change their color from dark greens to brilliant oranges and yellows, the blue-gray hills in the distance. I breathed in the sweet, fresh air of the land I loved, and I thought to myself, *This is life and it's a good life! It's here today and it's mine today—right this very moment. No one can tell me what tomorrow will bring, so today—today,* I reminded myself, *must be lived to its absolute fullest.*